Contents

1 Accounting for environmental sustainability – taking nature into account

2 Methodology – estimating a company's environmentally-sustainable profits

iv

References and further information

Appendices

List of abbreviations

ABI Association of British Insurers

BOD Biological Oxygen Demand

CERES Coalition of Environmentally Responsible Economies

CHP Combined Heat and Power

CNG Compressed Natural Gas

CO$_2$ Carbon Dioxide

COD Chemical Oxygen Demand

CSR Corporate Social Responsibility

DEFRA Department for the Environment, Food and Rural Affairs

DETR Department of the Environment, Transport and the Regions

EFS Environmental Financial Statement

EMS Environmental Management System

ETR Environmental/Ecological Tax Reform

EU European Union

GRI Global Reporting Initiative

HC Hydrocarbons

IPC Integrated Pollution Control

IPP Integrated Product Policy

IPPC Intergovernmental Panel on Climate Change

LPG Liquid Petroleum Gas

NGO Non-Government Organisation

NOx Nitrogen Oxides

OECD Organisation for Economic Co-operation and Development

PM Particulate Matter

PPP	Polluter Pays Principle
RCEP	Royal Commission on Environmental Pollution
SO$_2$	Sulphur Dioxide
SRI	Socially Responsible Investment
UNEP	United Nations Environment Programme
VOCs	Volatile Organic Compounds
WHO	World Health Organisation
WRI	World Resource Institute

List of boxes

List of figures

About the author

Rupert Howes is **Director** of **Forum for the Future's Sustainable Economy Programme (SEP).** He is a qualified chartered accountant (KPMG 1990) and has an MSc in Environmental Technology from Imperial College (1992) and a first degree in Economics (Sussex 1985).

Career history:
Research Fellow at the Science Policy Research Unit (SPRU) at Sussex University (1995–96).

Researcher at the International Institute for Environment and Development (IIED) (1992–95); freelance/consultancy experience with several other environment and development NGOs including WWF-International and the Institute for European Environmental Policy (IEEP).

He joined the Forum in January 1997. SEP projects currently include work on capital markets and the environment, the transformation of the UK energy sector, material/resource management and local and regional economic development. His own major research areas include corporate environmental and sustainability accounting and reporting, sustainable agriculture and integrated land use management, ecological tax reform/environmental taxation, and climate change.

In addition to leading the Programme, Rupert is a member of Forum's senior management team (SMT). He is a facilitator on the Cambridge Programme for Industry's & Forum for the Future's *Sustainability Learning Network (SLN)* programme (at Madingley in Cambridge) and sits on a number of advisory boards and panels.

About Forum for the Future

Forum for the Future is a UK-based sustainable development charity working in partnership with others to accelerate the transition to a sustainable future. With a staff of sixty-five and offices in London and Cheltenham, they have partnerships with businesses, local authorities, regional bodies and universities, working with them to help them deliver their commitment to sustainability. Forum provide advice and develop partnership work on issues as diverse as climate change, procurement strategies, environmental accounting and the digital divide. Forum also communicate what they learn with their partners to a wider network of decision-makers and opinion-formers and run a number of cutting edge projects engaging with a much wider audience in NGOs, business, higher education and government on key sustainable development challenges.

Foreword from Rt Hon Michael Meacher MP Minister of State (Environment)

As we move forward into the twenty-first century it is becoming increasingly clear that all sectors of society need to contribute to the task of delivering the four objectives of sustainable development:

- social progress which recognises the need of everyone;
- effective protection of the environment;
- prudent use of natural resources; and
- high and stable levels of economic growth and employment.

To make their contribution, organisations of all kinds need new tools to help them measure and manage their effect on sustainability. For some time now the Government has been encouraging companies and other organisations to measure, manage and report on their impact on the environment in terms of their water and energy use, and their greenhouse gas and waste emissions. This guide looks beyond these simple measurements to the new environmental accounting methodologies being developed to help organisations identify and cost, or 'internalise', their impact on the environment. It explores the various current approaches to the difficult task of identifying precisely what are the relevant externalities and describes in detail Forum for the Future's approach of looking at the 'sustainability costs' an organisation would need to spend 'to restore or avoid environmental damage'.

I welcome this guide as a most valuable contribution to the ongoing debate on the best way forward.

Michael Meacher

Rt Hon Michael Meacher MP
Minister of State (Environment)

Accounting for environmental sustainability – taking nature into account

1 Overview

This introductory guide to environmental accounting is divided into two parts. Part 1 provides an introduction to the dynamic subject of corporate environmental accounting. It outlines the business case and rationale for engaging in environmental accounting and illustrates how leading UK companies are already adding value and reducing risk through the use of innovative environmental accounting techniques and methodologies. The two broad focus areas of environmental accounting – accounting for 'internal' environmental-related expenditure (expenditure already incurred and captured within a company's accounting system but perhaps lost in general overheads) and 'external cost accounting' (the internalisation of environmental externalities) – are discussed. Part 1 also outlines the benefits associated with the public reporting of environmentally-related financial data.

The environmental accounting tool kit presented in Part 2 focuses on external cost accounting. The methodology detailed in this section provides a tool to estimate – within defined boundaries – the environmental sustainability of a company's activities and operations; in effect, the environmental sustainability of its economic activity. By linking monetarised environmental performance data to the company's mainstream financial and management accounting systems it attempts to quantify what could be considered as the organisation's environmentally sustainable profits. These are profits (or loss) that would remain at the end of an accounting period after provision has been made, or expenditure incurred, to restore or avoid the most significant external environmental impacts resulting from the company's activities and operations. A pro-forma set of external environmental cost accounts is presented together with a practical step-by-step guide to help individual organisations to begin the task of developing and drawing up their own external environmental cost accounts. Further guidance in the form of detailed data entry sheets (Green Sheets) developed by Forum for the Future to help organisations capture the necessary data to be able to produce their accounts is contained in Appendix 3.

The methodology presented has been developed by the sustainable development organisation Forum for the Future, a UK registered charity, with support from the Chartered Institute of Management Accountants (CIMA). The methodology has developed over several years and is already being used, and in some cases reported on, by several leading UK companies including Marks and Spencer, AWG (formally Anglian Water), Bulmers (the Herefordshire-based cider manufacturer), Interface Europe and Wessex Water. The guide draws on this case study experience to illustrate how other companies are approaching the task of developing their own environmental accounting systems to systematically deliver value and reduce business risk.

Whilst Part 1 provides useful contextual and background information it is not essential to read all of the individual sub-sections before reading the guidance in Part 2 on how to develop your own external cost accounts.

2 What is environmental accounting?

For the purposes of this guide, environmental accounting has been defined as:

The generation, analysis and use of monetarised environmentally-related information in order to improve corporate environmental and economic performance.

There are two main focuses: internal and external environmental accounting. Whilst this definition may seem a little dull, environmental accounting is not. It is all about making the link between environmental and financial performance more visible, getting 'environmental sustainability' embedded within an organisation's culture and operations, and providing decision-makers with the sort of information that can help them to reduce costs and business risk, and to add value.

It is a new area, with no hard and fast rules or standards. Only a few leading companies are actively engaged in environmental accounting but this is likely to change as the professional accounting bodies, financial analysts and other stakeholders begin to demand the disclosure and reporting of environmentally-related financial data to enable them to distinguish between good and bad performers. This transition is already beginning to happen, pushed along by several recent developments including the Company Law Review, the amendment to the 1995 Pensions Act, the Turnbull Report on internal controls and the recent Association of British Insurers (ABI) Guidelines on Socially Responsible Investing (SRI) (*see* Box 1 for more details on these and other regulatory and voluntary drivers).

Box 1: The mainstreaming of environmental and sustainability issues – implications for directors and investor relations

Several recent legislative developments, together with a number of voluntary initiatives and guidelines on reporting and public disclosure, have dramatically increased the pressure on all companies to manage and report the non-financial risks – including environmental, social and ethical risks – associated with their business activities. The most important of these are listed below together with a very brief overview of four of these important developments:

- The Combined Code and the Turnbull Report.

- The Company Law Review.

- DEFRA's Making A Corporate Commitment initiative.

- The Pensions Act disclosure measures.

- The Myners Review.

- The ABI guidelines on Socially Responsible Investment (SRI).

The Combined Code and the Turnbull Report: These complementary reports have been instrumental in recent improvements in corporate governance, both good practice and disclosure. Their effectiveness in driving change comes from a requirement to disclose compliance with the principles or an explanation of why not, as a requirement of London Stock Exchange listing. The Turnbull Report (1999) makes the link between sustainability and business success by taking a risk-based approach to internal controls. Guidance is provided on managing significant business risks from both hazards and missed opportunities, and encompasses non-financial as well as financial risks. Where exposure to non-financial risks, such as environmental and sustainability issues, are material to business value, the Turnbull guidance requires disclosure of what controls have been put in place. The Combined Code (1998) sets out principles and a code on the appropriate role of directors, their remuneration, relations with shareholders and accountability. Of particular importance is its requirement that companies should be ready to enter into a dialogue with their institutional shareholders on these issues and that institutional shareholders have a responsibility to make considered use of their votes.

The Company Law Review: *The Company Law Review* (2001) is intended to provide an orderly framework for the responsible and honest conduct of business by companies listed in the UK. Draft legislation is expected in

2002. Two key aspects to this legislation will be disclosure by companies of factors affecting future business performance, including environmental and community impacts, and the disclosure by institutional shareholders of their voting policy and actions. Proposals include the recommendation for companies to publish an expanded Operating and Financial Review (OFR). Among other things, the OFR will 'provide a review of the business, its performance, plans and prospects, and information the directors judge necessary for the understanding of the business, such as relationships with employees, suppliers and customers, environmental and community impacts, corporate governance and management of risk'.

The Pensions Act disclosure measures: One of the potentially most influential disclosure initiatives has been the amendment to the 1995 Pensions Act in 2000 (which came into force on 3 July 2001). Occupational and Local Authority pension funds control financial assets totalling almost £800 billion and, along with life insurance companies, are the major long-term investor in the UK economy. The amendments to the 1995 Pensions Act require pension fund trustees to disclose in their Statement of Investment Principles:

- the extent (if at all) to which social, environmental or ethical considerations are taken into account in the selection, retention and realisation of investments; and

- their policy (if any) in relation to the exercise of the rights (including voting rights) attaching to investments.

The ABI Guidelines on SRI: The other major institutional investor in the UK is the life insurance sector, which manages almost £1000 billion of assets. Recently, the Association of British Insurers (ABI) issued guidelines on SRI (2001) to their members, which look set to become the model for institutional investors. The guidelines were supported by a number of mainstream institutions and, if widely adopted, will herald a step change in investor engagement on sustainability issues. The key innovation is making an explicit link between sustainability issues and business value. The guidelines require companies to state in their annual report whether there is board-level commitment, policies and procedures that 'identify and assess the significant risks to the company's short- and long-term value from social, environmental and ethical matters, as well as opportunities to enhance value that might arise from an appropriate response'. Investors, using these guidelines, will be looking for evidence of how directors' incentives, training and systems lead to the effective management of these non-financial risks.

The Pensions Act disclosure requirements, Myners review and ABI guidelines on SRI promote active institutional investor engagement with the companies in which they are investing in relation to their environmental, social and ethical performance. Consequently, finance directors and investor relations departments, if they are not already doing so, will increasingly have to incorporate a review of these issues and how their companies are dealing with them to reduce risk and add value in their communications with financial stakeholders.

The UK Government is also applying further pressure on companies to improve and report on their environmental, ethical and social policy through a policy of 'naming and shaming' FTSE 250 companies that are currently not reporting. The disclosure of environmentally-related financial data is actively being encouraged and mandatory environmental reporting has been threatened and seems inevitable in the absence of more widespread and comprehensive reporting by UK companies. It has recently been introduced in France and is already in place in several other European countries.

If a company is seriously committed to the idea of decreasing its environmental footprint (the damage caused by its activities and operations), it needs to manage and control both its internal environmental costs (the costs relating to waste management, energy consumption, etc.) and begin to reduce the external environmental costs resulting from its activities. These costs are currently borne by the rest of society and represent 'value extracted' by the company, but not paid for.

The following sections provide more detail on these two aspects of environmental accounting, drawing on practical UK case study examples to illustrate how leading companies are already incorporating environmental accounting techniques and methodologies within their management information systems.

2.1 Internal environmental cost accounting

For a company embarking on environmental accounting, the identification of internal environmental costs provides a useful starting point. These costs can include the following:

- costs of monitoring emissions;
- licence, permits and authorisation costs;
- special insurance fees to cover the use of hazardous chemicals;
- payment of fines and charges;
- costs of operating an environmental department;
- capital spending with an environmental component.

There is no one definition of what constitutes environmentally-related expenditure and the importance of various categories will clearly vary depending upon the nature of the company and its principal activities. A more rigorous allocation of these costs can bring many benefits in itself. Often, environmental costs are hidden in overheads or allocated somewhat arbitrarily across departments/cost centres. Studies such as the World Resource Institute's (WRI) Green Ledgers (Ditz *et al.*, 1995) have shown that these costs can be substantial. The six case studies presented in the WRI study show that for certain products and facilities, environmental costs can account for 20 per cent of total costs.

When environmental costs are this significant, tighter and more transparent accounting can more than pay for itself. Traditional cost allocation methods (on the basis of machine hours, output or perhaps headcount) can lead to a situation where products with relatively low environmental costs subsidise those with higher costs. This results in poor product pricing decisions, as managers respond to distorted internal 'price signals'. The case of Spectrum Glass, one of the companies reviewed in the WRI study, illustrates this point. Their principal environmental concern was the use of the colourant cadmium oxide, a chemical used for only one product: 'ruby red' glass. This product is responsible for the bulk of the hazardous waste produced by the company. At the time of the study, with environmental costs being allocated across all products, 'ruby red' glass appeared profitable. However, if pending legislation on the release of cadmium takes effect, the company will discontinue the production of 'ruby red' glass.

Spectrum Glass may not be typical of the ease with which environmental costs are directly attributable to particular products. But it is indicative of how internal subsidies, created through a misallocation of costs, can lead to inappropriate pricing and product mix decisions. With more transparent and complete accounting, firms are more likely to be able to identify cost-saving opportunities, make better decisions with regard to product mix and pricing, and also be able to avoid future costs through inappropriate investment decisions. At the very least, making the link between environmental and financial performance more apparent can make it easier to take and win support for further environmental initiatives.

One way of presenting how value can be added through environmental investments and initiatives is through the preparation and reporting of a company-wide Environmental Financial Statement (EFS). The EFS is a periodic financial statement that attempts to collate and report, in a single statement, total environmental expenditure and any associated financial savings achieved as a result of that expenditure over the particular accounting period under review. The statement aims to capture all relevant items of environmentally-related expenditure, irrespective of which department or cost centre incurred them, and to match the expenditure, on a line-by-line basis, where appropriate, with its associated financial benefits or savings. A pro-forma EFS is shown in Figure 1.

Figure 1: Pro-forma Environmental Financial Statement (EFS)

	2002	2000
Environmental costs	**£**	**£**
Costs of basic programme		
Environmental services (percentage of)	X	X
Environmental/energy co-ordinators, etc.	X	X
Business unit environmental programmes and initiatives (including personnel costs/professional fees, etc.)	X	X
Waste minimisation and pollution prevention – operations and maintenance	X	X
Waste minimisation and pollution prevention – depreciation	X	X
Total cost of basic programme	**X**	**X**

Figure 1: Pro-forma Environmental Financial Statement (EFS) cont.

	2002	2000
Remediation, waste and other costs[1]		
Fines and prosecutions	X	X
Waste disposal costs	X	X
Environmental taxes – e.g. landfill, climate levy	X	X
Remediation/clean up costs	X	X
Other costs, etc.	X	X
Total remediation, waste and other costs	X	X
Total environmental costs	**X**	**X**
Environmental savings		
Income, savings, and cost avoidance from report year	X	X
Reduced insurance from avoidance of hazardous materials	X	X
Reduced landfill tax and other waste disposal costs	X	X
Energy conservation savings	X	X
Water conservation savings	X	X
Reduced packaging savings	X	X
Income from sale of recovered and recycled materials	X	X
Other savings, etc.	X	X
Total environmental savings	**X**	**X**
As a percentage of environmental costs	*X*	*X*
Summary of Savings		
Savings in report year	X	X
Savings brought forward from initiatives in prior years	X	X
Total income, savings and cost avoidance	**X**	**X**

1 – Proactive environmental action will clearly minimise these costs and hence reduce the 'cost' side of the statement.

Until recently only one company, Baxter Healthcare Corporation, a US company, has attempted to produce and report a company-wide EFS. Baxter spent several years developing the EFS methodology and recognises that the process and procedure has evolved and developed considerably since it first engaged in corporate environmental accounting in the early 1990s. When cumulative savings brought forward are taken into account, Baxter's have found that savings and avoided costs from environmental investments actually exceed environmentally-related expenditure. As noted on the company's web site, in 1999, environmental investments instituted in prior years back to 1992 yielded approximately $86 million in savings and cost avoidance. 'Our experience makes a powerful bottom-line argument for environmentally-responsible corporate behaviour that should appeal even to companies that haven't yet made environmental issues a priority.' (www.baxter.com). In the reporting year 1999, savings of $12 million equated to 80 per cent of the costs of the basic environmental programme.

More recently, in the UK, the construction services company Carillion has been working with Forum for the Future on the development of a pilot EFS for one of the company's private finance initiative (PFI) projects – the Dartford and Gravesham hospital in Kent. The draft EFS produced for Carillion and published in their 2000 Environmental and Community Report is reproduced in Figure 2. Other companies are also beginning to develop and produce their own Environmental Financial Statements. Working with Forum, Bulmers produced a company-wide EFS in 2002 as part of the company's attempt to develop and report on its 'triple bottom line' performance, i.e. its economic, social and environmental performance over the accounting period under review. In the same year, Wessex Water produced an EFS for a single business asset – its membrane sewage treatment works at Swanage, Dorset. Wessex Water intends to follow Bulmers example of producing a company-wide EFS over the coming years.

Figure 2: The Dartford and Gravesham Special Project's Environmental Financial Statement
(covering the three-year construction phase to April 2000)

Environmental costs	£
Payroll and labour costs	
Apportionment of technical services manager's and others' time	60,000
Other costs?	X
Costs of basic programme	60,000
Remediation, waste and other costs	
Waste disposal costs	250,000
Tree protection – metal fencing	7,500
Environmental taxes paid – landfill tax, other costs, etc.	X
Total remediation, waste and other costs	257,500
Total environmental costs	317,500
Environmental savings	
Income, savings, and cost avoidance	
Ground stabilisation – net savings building materials avoided	111,500
Re-use of excavated material on site – fuel costs avoided	–
Avoided landfill charges/waste disposal costs	50,000
Construction of drainage swale – avoided drainage infrastructure costs	20,000
Reduced landfill tax and other waste disposal costs	X
Income from sale of recovered and recycled materials (see notes)	
Other savings, etc.	X
Total environmental savings	181,500
As a percentage of environmental costs	57%

Selected notes

Ground stabilisation: The net saving shown in the statement of £111,500 represents half of the total savings achieved from avoiding the use of some 26,000m³ of type 1 granular and capping material. The saving was shared with the contractor involved in the stabilisation work. In addition to the savings shown in the EFS, nearly 2000 wagon/lorry journeys were also avoided – resulting in reduced emissions of carbon dioxide and less noise and disturbance for the local community.

Drainage swale: The construction of a drainage swale in place of conventional drainage infrastructure for the site was estimated to save in the region of £20,000 in construction costs. There are several additional benefits, not shown in the EFS, associated with the construction of the swale. Surface run-off and drainage water is diverted from going to sewer and instead flows into the swale recharging the aquifer. A number of petrol interceptors ensure that petrol, oil and other contaminants are removed from the water before it reaches the swale. The reduced volume of water going to sewer also means a reduced volume of waste water needing energy-intensive waste water treatment (saving costs for the local water company) and hence also helps to avoid yet more emissions of carbon dioxide.

Bulk excavation: During construction some 46,000m³ of spoil was excavated along with 28,700m³ of top soil and head deposit material. All of this material was re-used on site avoiding a potential landfill tax bill of £373,500. In addition, the fuel costs alone of transporting this material to a landfill site would have exceeded £35,500 (from nearly 5000 lorry/wagon journeys). Given that on-site re-use of excavated material is becoming standard practice, these substantial avoided costs have not been included in the EFS. From an environmental perspective, the key benefit resulting from this successful 'cut and fill' exercise was the fact that very little additional/new building materials had to be imported onto site. Other benefits include avoided emissions of carbon dioxide and less noise and disturbance to the communities living around the site.

Source: *We are Making Choices*, Carillion's Environment, Community and Social Accounting Report 2000.

As shown in the Dartford and Gravesham project EFS, financial savings were estimated at £181,500 or 57 per cent of estimated environmentally-related costs. Whilst costs still outweigh savings, the magnitude of cost-avoidance opportunities identified are still significant. They are also likely to be an underestimate as a number of potentially material savings, such as reduced waste water costs resulting from the construction of a drainage swale have not been quantified (see the notes to the statement in Figure 2).

One of the aims of producing an EFS is to demonstrate that environmental initiatives can generate an income and save money, i.e. an environmental programme is not a constraint on business performance but could actually make a positive contribution. This was demonstrated at Dartford and Gravesham. In an effort to reduce waste costs, for example, and to maximise the re-use of waste materials generated, a policy of segregating waste materials into single material bins was employed throughout the construction phase of the project. Of the 3400 tonnes of waste generated, some 1900 (55 per cent) was segregated in this way. In the absence of this segregation, which resulted in metal waste, for example, being collected at no cost, total waste disposal costs would have been some £50,000 higher. Consequently the process of preparing the statement can help to find and highlight examples of best practice and cost-saving opportunities that can then be replicated across the company – enhancing profits and reducing impacts. It can also contribute to the identification of inappropriate methods of cost allocation that may be leading to inappropriate/sub-optimal decisions. The EFS can also focus attention on environmental priorities, win support for environmental actions, catalyse debate and motivate the search for innovative solutions.

Other innovative environmental accounting initiatives include ongoing work by the Co-operative Bank investigating the link between their ethical policies and the bank's overall profitability. In the reporting year 2000, 15–18 per cent of the bank's pre-tax profits were attributed to the Co-operative Bank's brand and reputation (see their web page at www.co-operativebank.co.uk or their latest Partnership Report for details). Similarly, work by Envirowise, a government programme to help companies increase their profitability through increasing their resource productivity also suggested that environmental accounting can help companies to find hidden value. With funding from CIMA, ACCA, the Environment Agency, DEFRA and the Institute of Chartered Accountants in England and Wales (ICAEW), Envirowise have produced a guide for business *Using Environmental Management Accounting to Increase Profits*. The publication was launched in May 2002.

Internal costs, however, are just one part of the equation. The next essential step for a company committed to moving towards environmental sustainability is to begin to account for its external environmental impacts. The rationale for internalising these externalities and the business case for doing so are presented below. Part 2 then moves on to detail how individual organisations can begin the task of producing their own external cost accounts.

2.2 External cost accounting – internalising environmental externalities

Whilst companies 'add value' through their activities they also extract value for which they do not pay. Their activities and operations give rise to external environmental impacts such as the contamination of ground water, traffic congestion, poor urban air quality and so on. The costs of these external impacts are picked up by the rest of society, prices do not reflect costs and as such companies (and individuals) do not pay the full costs of their production and consumption decisions. Instead sub-optimal and inefficient decisions are made as producers and consumers respond to imperfect price signals. At the level of an individual company this means that profits as reported may not be environmentally sustainable. The degree to which the company is genuinely 'adding value' through its activities remains uncertain and if the company was to pay a dividend, the payment could end up being made out of natural capital rather than income – a situation which is clearly unsustainable over the long term. See Box 2 and Appendix 2 for a more detailed explanation.[2] The assumption that the company is a 'going concern' may also no longer be valid.

Box 2: The maintenance of natural capital: something is missing from corporate accounts

Can wealth-creation and environmental sustainability ever be reconciled or is there an inherent conflict between profits and the environment? Much of the business school rhetoric, from the late 1980s to the present day, would suggest there is no conflict. The talk is all of 'win-win' or 'double dividend' opportunities, measures that bring reduced environmental impact and enhanced profitability. Clean and efficient industries, it is said, will produce new products and technologies without environmental destruction. But despite their obvious appeal, the adoption of clean technology, waste minimisation and the pursuit of energy and eco-efficiency in isolation will never be enough. While these activities need to be encouraged and actively promoted, given the magnitude of the environmental challenges we face, it would be naïve to rely on what industry deems to be 'win-win' to deliver necessary environmental improvements. Producing more from less is not the same as sustainable industrial production.

The role of natural capital

The problem, in part, stems from the failure of accounting systems – at the national level and at the corporate level – to fully account for 'natural' capital. While companies account for the depreciation of manufactured capital, to ensure that productive capacity and hence the ability to generate future returns and income is maintained, no account is made for the degradation of natural capital when calculating corporate profits. Natural capital can be thought of as the exploitable resources of the earth's ecosystem, its oceans, forests, mountains and plains, that provide the raw material inputs, resources and flows of energy into our production processes. It also consists of a range of 'ecosystem services'. These services include the provision of an atmosphere and a stable climate, a protective ozone layer, and the absorptive capacities to disperse, neutralise and recycle the material outputs and pollution generated in ever increasing quantities from our global economic activities. While some account is taken of the depletion of resources, no account is taken of the degradation of what has been described as 'critical natural capital', the essential ecosystem services without which no life, let alone economic activity, would exist.

Evidence of this incomplete accounting is abundant. For example, while companies may account for the timber (i.e. the actual resource) which they extract from a forest, they do not account for the ecosystem services provided by that forest. These include water storage, soil stability, habitat and the regulation of the atmosphere and climate. Unfortunately, the cost of these essential ecosystem services become all too apparent when they start to break down. In China's Yangtze basin in 1998, for example, deforestation triggered flooding that killed 3700 people, dislocated 223 million and inundated 60 million acres of farmland. This $30 billion disaster forced a logging moratorium and a $12 billion emergency reforestation programme (Lovins et al., 1999). Similarly, external costs of global climate change are beginning to become more obvious. Storm and extreme weather event-related damage (global climate change is expected to increase the frequency and severity of such events) caused upwards of $90 billion of damage in 1998 alone. This represents more weather-related damage destruction than reported in the entire decade of the 1980s (Lovins et al., 1999).

The key to resolving the conflict between profits and the environment, as many have pointed out, lies in getting the prices right. Businesses (and consumers) should pay for the external costs of their activities; farmers should pay for the contamination of ground water (and not be subsidised to pollute the water in the first place); timber companies should pay for the destruction of water catchments; and industry should pay for its myriad external environmental impacts. These include industry's contribution to global climate change, its impact on poor and declining urban air quality, loss of agricultural production and productivity as a result of aqueous and gaseous emissions and direct impacts, and disposal of waste to land. Until this happens, the conflict will remain. Only when these costs have been internalised will profits, as reported in financial accounts, approximate to what can be regarded as environmentally *sustainable* profits. One way of getting the prices right is through the process of ecological tax reform (ETR); i.e. moving taxes from the good elements, such as employment and profits, to the bad elements of resource use and pollution. The UK's landfill tax and the climate change levy are examples of ETR. The revenues raised from these taxes are redistributed back into the economy by reducing employers' National Insurance (NI) contributions. However, neither of these taxes fully reflects the full extent of the external impacts resulting from the disposal of waste or the business use of fossil fuel-derived energy.

In the absence of the political will to establish a comprehensive and radical ETR programme, companies committed to improving their environmental performance need to move beyond simple corporate environmental reporting, to begin to account more completely and transparently for both their internal environmental costs and their external impacts. In effect, they need to begin to account for the depreciation of 'natural capital' in the same way that accounting rules and standards require them to account for the depreciation of manufactured capital. Once these costs are internalised, everything changes: prices, costs and what is or is not profitable.

Source: Howes, R (2000). Corporate Environmental Accounting: Accounting for Environmentally Sustainable Profits, in *Greening the Accounts,* part of the *Current Issues in Ecological Economics* series, *eds J Proops and S Simon, Edward Elgar Publishers, UK, 2000.*

For a company committed to moving towards environmental sustainability, the challenge is to try and determine/estimate what its environmentally-sustainable profits may be and hence to gauge to what extent it is really adding value and making the transition to becoming a more environmentally-sustainable enterprise. The development of more complete, transparent and integrated accounts/accounting systems – systems that specifically take into account the most significant external environmental impacts resulting from a company's operations – is a prerequisite to enable a company to be able to do this. As noted, several UK companies including AWG, Wessex Water, Marks and Spencer, and Bulmers, have already embarked on developing such systems. The methodology detailed in Part 2 is based on the approach being taken and developed by these companies.

3   The business case

The long-term future and sustainability of individual corporations is inescapably linked to their ability to reduce their environmental impacts and to continuously improve their overall environmental (and social) performance. Leading companies recognise this. For example, Wessex Water, in their 2001 Annual Review and Accounts, state that 'in the long term, the 'bottom line' is that all economic value flows from products and services provided by the environment (natural capital) and people (human capital) themselves. These resources should not be eroded; instead a sustainable society would live off what can be provided year after year.'[3] Similarly, in their 2001 Sustainable Development Report, *Transforming our World*, AWG states that the integration of sustainable development into a company's activities and operations will bring advantages to the business as well as to the environment and the communities within which that business is operating.[4]

What were once external costs can quickly become internalised through environmental regulation and taxes. The landfill tax, climate change levy and aggregates taxes provide recent examples of such legislation. Governments throughout Europe are committed to the increased use of such policy instruments. Customer and local community's expectations and demands for responsible corporate environmental governance are also increasing and the consequences of corporate 'environmental and/or social failure' (for example, Shell with the disposal of Brent Spar and Nike with child labour) have become all too apparent.

Financial stakeholders are also showing more interest in assessing corporate environmental performance. Whilst investor/financial market pressure has historically been limited to concern over legal liabilities and to negative risk factors, recent legislative changes (see Box 1, pp. 5–7), and emerging evidence of the link between earnings and environmental management have encouraged analysts to consider the more positive aspects of corporate environmental performance. Increasingly the quality of a company's environmental management is being seen as an indicator to the outside world of the overall quality of its management – a key investment/stock selection consideration. Analysts are being urged to demand new forms of data and information to measure this more positive aspect of corporate environmental governance. A number of commercial environmental risk-rating methodologies and several new financial products based on an assessment of environmental/sustainability performance (such as the FTSE4Good indices, Dow Jones Sustainability Group Index and others) have been launched in response to this demand. The ability to compare and benchmark performance is becoming increasingly important. Environmental accounting, involving the monetarisation/valuation of environmental impacts and their integration into mainstream corporate accounting, could, potentially, be one of the tools/methodologies to enable such comparisons to be made.

Being aware of their environmental costs (and benefits), i.e. the company's exposure to potential environmental problems (before they become issues), can assist the company's management in its forward/strategic planning and consequently help to reduce the company's exposure to future environmental risks and liabilities. Without

19

adequate and appropriate systems to identify and account for such costs it is unlikely that companies will be able to meet the future expectations of their customers, shareholders and, as noted in Box 1, the requirements of a more stringent regulatory environment and environmentally aware City.[5] 'First movers' will clearly have an advantage.

4 The benefits of reporting

The preparation and public reporting of a set of external environmental cost accounts (and/or an EFS) can also contribute to meeting the increasing demands from external audiences for environmentally-related financial data. Whilst the City is not interested in reactive, ad hoc environmental initiatives, it is interested when a company can demonstrate a systematic approach to delivering consistently greater value and reducing business risk through effective environmental management. Environmental cost accounts and/or an EFS and its supporting accounting system can contribute to providing relevant data for this purpose. The public reporting of environmental accounts can also serve as a powerful demonstration of a company's overall commitment to managing and reducing its environmental impacts. Publication can therefore provide an effective means for companies to differentiate themselves in increasingly competitive global markets and thereby help them to secure existing markets and contribute to winning new business, attract and retain the best employees, and maintain their 'license to operate' within the communities where they are based. It could also contribute to increasing the demand for the company's share capital and lowering its cost of borrowing as investors are encouraged to seek out and invest in 'best in sector' (in terms of their overall financial, social and environmental performance) companies.

Footnotes

2 – The appendices also provide an explanation on the difference between 'sustainability' and 'sustainable development', what do they actually mean? – Disentangling the Definitions, Sustainability and Sustainable Development

3 – *Wessex Water Services Ltd Annual Review and Accounts 2001: Tap into your water source* (page 61). The external cost accounts can help companies to define what can be provided year after year, i.e. to define these limits and to identify the options that are available to the company to enable it to reduce its external footprint and to begin to make the transition towards environmental sustainability

4 – *Transforming our world: Sustainable Development Report 2001*. AWG010/6/01. The report defines these advantages as follows: winning business – by creating additional advantages and opportunities; reducing costs – by introducing efficiencies which directly reduce our consumption of resources and are attractive to the investment community; reducing risk – developing and contributing to sustainable regulation and competition, and becoming even better managers of corporate risk; and growing the business – developing and applying new technology

5 – By identifying external environmental risks, and the opportunities open to the company to avoid or reduce them, external cost accounting can also contribute to helping companies meet their obligations under the Combined Code to establish adequate systems of internal control.

The methodology – estimating a company's environmentally-sustainable profits

1 Overview

Accounting for environmental externalities is a new and emerging area of corporate environmental accounting. There are no hard and fast rules and each stage of the methodology is associated with its own particular challenges and issues. Despite this, several leading UK companies are now applying a consistent methodology and approach to accounting for their external environmental impacts.

This section provides an overview of this methodology. Pro-forma external cost accounts are presented and the key stages involved in producing periodic external cost accounts are discussed. Some of the methodologically difficult areas involved – particularly with regard to where the system boundaries are drawn and the approach to environmental valuation (one of the key stages) – are also considered.

The section concludes by providing detailed guidance on how organisations can approach the task of producing their own external cost accounts. Each of the individual cost line entries shown in the pro-forma accounts are reviewed in turn. Further guidance in the form of detailed data entry sheets (Green Sheets) developed by Forum for the Future to help organisations capture the necessary data to be able to produce their accounts is provided in Appendix 3. The Green Sheets (a term coined by one of the companies engaged in the development of the methodology) have been designed to capture both the physical quantitative information required to estimate, for example, emissions of carbon dioxide from the consumption of gas, and also the associated financial data. The capture of environmentally-related financial data can provide the starting point for developing a company-wide Environmental Financial Statement (EFS). The sheets also provide suggestions of possible data sources.

The Appendices also contain a Pro-Forma Expense Form (see Appendix 4) designed and used by Forum for the Future to ensure our own accounting system captures all of the necessary information we require to produce our own external cost accounts routinely. As shown, Forum uses different cost codes for each mode of travel – by air, train, car and taxi, etc. Reports can be run as and when required to provide total mileage by mode of travel (and also total mileage by mode, by person, or department as required). This information together with additional data on our use of electricity, gas, etc. (also captured and isolated within the accounting system) provides the basis for producing our external cost accounts each year. (Forum's latest environmental external cost accounts can be seen on our web page – www.forumforthefuture.org.uk.)

2 Aims and objectives of the methodology

The methodology detailed in this section provides a tool to estimate, within narrow system boundaries, the environmental sustainability of a company's activities and operations. In effect the environmental sustainability of its economic activity. By linking monetarised environmental performance data to the company's mainstream financial and management accounting systems it attempts to quantify what could be considered, again within the narrow system boundaries adopted, as the organisation's environmentally sustainable profits.[6] These are profits (or loss) that would remain at the end of an accounting period after provision has been made, or expenditure incurred, to restore or avoid the most significant external environmental impacts resulting from the company's activities and operations; in essence, to estimate the profit level that would remain if the company endeavoured to leave the plant in a similar state at the end of the accounting period as it had been at the beginning of that period. The methodology presented is already being used (and in some cases being reported) by Interface, Bulmers, Wessex Water, AWG and Marks and Spencer.

As for most things, the devil is very much in the detail. Impacts need to be identified and captured:

- Which impacts do you include, which do you exclude and where do you draw the system boundaries (i.e. to what degree are life cycle impacts accounted for)? Once impacts have been identified how do you translate them into emissions?
- Do generic conversion factors exist and where can they be found?
- Once the impacts to be included have been found how do you determine an appropriate valuation to use in the accounts?
- What are the options?

This brief introduction and guide cannot provide comprehensive answers to all of these questions. However, each illustrative heading in the pro-forma accounts is considered in turn and the issues identified above are addressed as much as possible. A number of relevant publications, articles and information sources are also listed at the end of the section for those who want more information and greater detail. The guide should be more than sufficient to get organisations started on the process of engaging in environmental accounting and to enable them, with further reference and information as required, to be able to draw up draft environmental accounts for themselves.

3   The sustainability cost estimate – what does it actually mean?

The sustainability cost estimate for a company's activities, as shown in the pro-forma accounts, is simply the summation of all of the various quantified and valued environmental impacts. It represents the calculated cost to the company to reduce its environmental impacts to a socially acceptable and sustainable level.[7] The principal purpose of the estimation is to illustrate what a given/stated improvement in environmental quality would cost. Market prices are used wherever possible. To facilitate the ability to compare sustainability cost estimations (and or environmentally-sustainable profit figures) between years and between different companies, institutional incentives (in the form of grants and rebates) together with potential savings available if avoidance options are adopted should be excluded from the accounts. Although of immense importance in terms of decision-making, such incentives may change overnight and hence comparative figures from prior years could become meaningless in later periods. Consequently, the estimation simply represents the cost of achieving a given improvement in environmental quality based on current (and available) technology. In this 'pure' form, the sustainability cost estimate (to achieve consistent standards or improvements in environmental quality) will only change for two reasons: changes in absolute emissions/impacts (which will hopefully be decreasing) or from changes in abatement technology (and the price of that technology).

When deducted from the company's financial profits as reported in the main annual report and accounts, an estimate of what could be considered as the company's environmentally-sustainable profits is obtained. It is this linking of the monetarised environmental performance data to the mainstream financial accounting (and or management accounting) system that is the key innovation in the methodology. Senior managers and directors are familiar with traditional accounting and reporting systems, and by integrating monetarised impact data in this way, the methodology provides:

- an easily understood take on what the external costs and negative impacts of the company's operations are; and more importantly,
- an indication of what it would cost the company to get its operations onto a more sustainable trajectory and a base line upon which to measure progress year on year.

Anglian Water, for example, in their 2001 sustainability report *Transforming Our World*, published the headline sustainability cost estimates for three consecutive accounting periods (for the years 1999–2001). As shown in Figure 3, the report also shows the impact of the sustainability cost estimates on the company's financial performance for the three years under review. Although the annual results are not directly comparable, it can be seen that the sustainability cost estimate, as a percentage of post tax profits, increased over the three years: from £15.55 million (8.1 per cent of post tax profits as originally reported) in 1999 to £16.4 million (11.9 per cent of post tax profits as originally reported) in 2001. The increase is largely explained by a significant increase in the consumption of fossil fuel-derived electricity to meet higher water quality standards over the period.

Figure 3: Anglian Water Services adjusted profit and loss (highlights) for the three accounting years ending 31 March 1999, 2000 and 2001

	1999[8]	2000	2001
	£000's	£000's	£000's
			(provisional)
Turnover	743,100	731,500	694,600
Sustainability cost of operations	*(15,550)*	*(16,100)*	*(16,400)*
Total other operating costs (as reported)	(419,400)	(431,700)	(429,400)
Revised operating profit	308,150	283,700	248,800
Revised profit on ordinary activities after taxation	177,050	153,100	121,500
Dividends	(326,000)	(148,900)	(124,200)
Revised movement in reserves	**(148,950)**	**4,200**	**(2,700)**
	1999	2000	2001
Impact on profits (compared to post-tax profits as originally reported)	8.1%	9.5%	11.9%

4 How to get started

The four key stages required to develop a set of external cost accounts are as follows:

1. The setting of system boundaries and subsequent identification/confirmation of the company's most significant/major environmental impacts to include within the accounts.

2. The establishment/estimation of appropriate 'sustainability targets'.

3. The valuation of identified impacts on the basis of what it would cost to avoid them in the first place or if avoidance is not possible, what it would cost to restore any resulting damage (using market-based prices as much as possible).

4. The development of a set of environmental accounts incorporating the external costs/sustainability cost of the company's activities.

As noted, it is this last step, the linking of monetarised corporate environmental performance data to the company's financial accounting system (to estimate the company's environmentally-sustainable/adjusted profits) that represents the main innovation in the methodology. The pro-forma accounts in Figure 4 and Wessex Water's external cost accounts for the accounting period to 31 March 2001 (see Figure 5) illustrate how this can be achieved. Wessex published their 2001 external cost accounts in the main annual review and accounts for that year. The extract from Anglian's report above illustrates how making the link between a company's financial and external environmental performance can also be achieved through the reporting of key/headline figures alone. Sections 4.2 to 4.4 discuss the issue of sustainability targets, the approach to impact identification and impact valuation. But first the next section considers the issue of system boundaries.

Figure 4: Pro-forma consolidated external environmental cost accounts for A Company PLC for the period 30 April 2002

Emissions/impacts *(selected account headings)*	Emissions (Tonnes)	Unit Cost (£) (where relevant)	£000s *'to deliver the relevant sutainability targets'*
Impacts to air			
Direct energy			
Natural gas consumption kWhs		Avoidance and restoration costs	
CO_2	X	X	
NOx, SO_2	X	X	
Total			X
Electricity consumption kWh			
CO_2	X	X	
NOx, SO_2	X	X	
Total (avoidance)			X
Production-related emissions			
VOCs	X	X	
NOx, SO_2, etc.	X	X	X
Transport			
Company cars, kms			
CO_2	X	X	
NOx, HCs and particulates	X	X	
Total company cars			X
Freight/distribution and contractors, kms			
CO_2	X	X	
NOx, HCs and particulates	X	X	
Total distribution			X
Air miles/aviation			

Emissions/impacts *(selected account headings)*	Emissions (Tonnes)	Unit Cost (£) (where relevant)	£000s *'to deliver the relevant sutainability targets'*
Impacts to air *(continued)*			
CO$_2$	X	X	
NOx	X	X	
Impacts to land			
Waste disposal to landfill	X	X	X
Contaminated land (restoration)			X
Impacts to water			
Abstraction at vulnerable sites			X
Total sustainability cost			**X**
Profit after tax per the financial accounts			X
Environmentally-sustainable/adjusted profit			**X**

Figure 5: Wessex Water Services external environmental cost accounts for the year to 31 March 2001

Emissions/impacts	Emissions (Tonnes)	Reduction Target (Tonnes) (sustainability gap)	Unit cost (£)(where relevant)	£000's to deliver the targets
Impacts to air				
Direct energy Electricity consumption 195.1 million kWh CO_2	86,325	51,741	–	
NOx	234	140	–	
SO_2	488	293	–	
Total (avoidance)				1,950
Natural gas consumption 11.07 million kWhs (CO_2 only)	2,103	1,262	6	8
Diesel Oil – 18.91 million litres CO_2 only	4,728	2,837	6	17
Production-related emissions Methane (CH_4) Emissions from waste water treatment	91,140 (Expressed as CO_2 equivalent)	54,684	6	328
Transport Company cars (petrol and diesel) 13.2 million kms				
CO_2	403	241	6	2
NOx, HCs and particulates	1	<1	14,000	8
Commercial vehicles (petrol and diesel) 13.2 million kms				
CO_2	3,918	2,381	6	14
NOx, HCs and particulates	30.5	17	7,200-14,000	323
Commuting and private car use 8.3 million kms				
CO_2	2,294	1,377	6	9
NOx, HCs and PM	16	8	7,200-14,000	100
Contractors, 11.4 million kms				
CO_2	2,500	1,500	6	10
NOx, HCs and PM	37	17	7,200-14,000	282
Total costs carried forward				*3051*

Emissions/impacts	Emissions (Tonnes)	Reduction Target (Tonnes) (sustainability gap)	Unit (£)(where relevant)	£000's to deliver the targets
Impacts to land				
Total costs brought forward				*3051*
Contaminated land (restoration of sacrificial and dedicated land)	–	6,000-9,000		120
Impacts to water				
Abstraction at vulnerable sites – provision of alternative supplies	–	–	–	5,170
Total sustainability cost				8,341
Profit after tax per the Financial Accounts				72,000
Environmentally sustainable /adjusted profit				63,659

4.1 System boundaries – the application of the polluter pays principle

One of the objectives of the methodology is to provide an estimate of the sustainability cost of the company over the accounting period under review that can be compared between accounting periods and also, eventually, between companies operating within, and also across, different sectors. The sustainability cost estimate, normalised as required, can then provide a useful generic indicator of the company's overall progress towards (or away from) environmental sustainability. To facilitate this, only direct or first level impacts (i.e. those for which a company is directly responsible for and has the greatest ability to control) are accounted for together with the second level impacts associated with the use of electricity. The inclusion of these upstream energy-related impacts ensures the methodology is consistent with the Government's (DETR's (now DEFRA's)) guidelines for the calculation and reporting of greenhouse gas emissions.[9]

In effect, the adoption of narrow system boundaries represents an attempt to apply the polluter pays principle to an individual company. If this principle were applied equitably and consistently, all other producers (and consumers) would be responsible for the direct environmental impacts resulting from their own production and consumption decisions. If they all calculated their own sustainability cost based on the same tight/narrow definition of system boundaries it would ensure that all significant external impacts are accounted for once and only once – there would be no danger of double counting. The methodology can incorporate wider life-cycle impacts but their inclusion could inhibit the comparability of the sustainability cost and environmentally-sustainable profit estimates between companies.[10]

Work with Interface, for example, has looked at extending the system boundaries used to draw up the company's external cost accounts to include the impacts associated with the manufacture of some of their principal raw material supplies – i.e. the incorporation of upstream life-cycle impacts. The materials looked at included nylon, PVC, bitumen and limestone fillers. Some of these inputs, nylon in particular, are associated with a very high-embodied energy content per unit of material. Consequently, their inclusion in the external cost accounts can increase the estimated sustainability cost calculation significantly. Whilst Interface found this additional life-cycle information useful for supply chain management purposes (for informing both their supplier and materials selection decisions), it decided not to incorporate it within the external cost accounts for the period under review. Instead, the implications of this additional life-cycle information were disclosed 'below the line'. Although related, supply chain management and the management of the company's direct environmental impacts were seen as distinct issues, each requiring discreet information flows to enable managers to make more informed decisions. The merging of these two issues was seen as having the potential to dilute and confuse the messages and implications coming out of the external cost accounting work and hence, as noted, the information flows were kept separate.

Similarly, current work with Marks and Spencer (in 2002) is examining how the downstream impacts associated with the consumption and final disposal of a number of product lines could be incorporated into the company's external cost accounting work. It seems likely that this will lead to the production of two sets of external cost statements: one focusing on internal/direct issues and impacts; and the other on the downstream life-cycle impacts. It is hoped that the results of this work will also be published and shared more widely when completed.

The use of narrow system boundaries can also be justified on the basis that it focuses on those impacts that the company has the greatest immediate ability to control and influence. However, it is important to note that without concerted action by everyone along the supply chain – producers of raw material inputs, processors, packers, distributors, and final consumers, etc. – it would be inappropriate to consider the profits as reported by companies using this methodology as genuinely 'environmentally sustainable'. You cannot have a sustainable company operating in an unsustainable economy. Consequently, as shown in the pro-forma accounts in Figure 4 earlier it may be more appropriate to refer to the final profit figure disclosed in the accounts as 'environmentally adjusted' rather than 'environmentally sustainable'. This could help to prevent the likelihood of any misleading impressions/messages being given to the targeted audiences for any particular company's environmental accounts.

4.2 Sustainability targets and closing the 'sustainability gap'

Our current systems of industrial production and consumption are clearly unsustainable. As noted, we are overwhelming and destroying the productive capacity of the planet and the life-support systems upon which all life on earth, let alone economic activity, is dependent (see Box 2, pp. 16–18). Whilst there may be uncertainty over what constitutes a sustainable level of economic activity, one thing is certain, the transition towards a more sustainable economy will require a dramatic increase in the level of resource productivity – perhaps by a factor of four or more. We will need to produce more from less and dramatically decrease the amount of waste – solid, gaseous and liquid – generated within our industrial economies.

The external cost accounting methodology attempts to apply this notion of ecological limits when determining the appropriate sustainability targets for an individual company's impact/emission reduction targets:

- What are emissions now?
- What might a sustainable level of emissions look like? And hence;
- How big is the 'sustainability gap' between where we are now and where we need to get to?
- How are we going to close that gap?

In determining what level of impacts could be considered as 'socially acceptable' and 'sustainable', reference is made to the latest scientific thinking and understanding. For example, the Intergovernmental Panel on Climate Change (the IPCC) suggests that emissions of greenhouse gases need to be reduced by about 60 per cent (compared to their 1990 levels) in order to prevent dangerous anthropogenic interference of our climatic systems. The UK's Royal Commission on Environmental Pollution (RCEP) suggests that we need to reduce emissions by 60 per cent by 2050 to avoid dangerous climatic instability. Consequently, most companies using this methodology have adopted a 60 per cent reduction target, generally implemented in the year under review, as their sustainability target for their emissions of greenhouse gases. Some have adopted a zero sustainability target, aiming to avoid or offset 100 per cent of their carbon dioxide emissions.

Similarly, in relation to non-carbon transport or production-related emissions, reference has been made to current health based guidelines and standards for the various pollutants covered in the accounts. To meet World Health Organisation (WHO) air quality standards, for example, road transport emissions of NOx, amongst other pollutants, will probably need to be reduced by at least 50–60 per cent. This target will clearly vary across the world, depending upon the level of background pollution and current emission levels, but forms a reasonable basis for target setting.

However, it is important not to get stuck on the issue of targets. In reality, we do not know what a sustainable level of emissions or impacts may be, hence a pragmatic approach is required when setting targets, as noted above, informed where possible by current knowledge and understanding. Individual companies may already have set their own targets for emission and impact reductions, and hence may want to use these as the basis for drawing up their external cost accounts. Whilst these targets may not be 'true sustainability targets' there is no reason for not using them as long as the notes to the accounts clearly state the reasoning and logic behind their selection and use, and that the targets themselves are clearly disclosed.

4.3   Identification of impacts

Impacts will vary between organisations and hence the headings in the environmental accounts will also vary. The headings included in the pro-forma accounts are illustrative but by no means comprehensive. Some entries are, however, likely to be common to all organisations – no matter what the precise nature of their activities or scale of their operations. These include emissions to air associated with the use of energy in offices and buildings – from electricity use and perhaps also gas, and the emissions associated with the use of energy in transportation, perhaps from company cars, distribution or simply from employees commuting to and from their regular place of employment. Other business-related travel might also be significant, for example air miles and rail miles. Impacts to other media are likely to be more relevant for some sectors than others. Impacts to water, for example and perhaps not surprisingly, were found to be very significant for the two water companies engaged in external cost accounting, particularly in relation to abstraction from low-flow rivers.

The pro-forma accounts have been drawn up to be consistent with the broad headings contained in the latest version of the *Global Reporting Initiative (GRI) Sustainability Reporting Guidelines* (see Box 3). See also the GRI web page at www.globalreporting.org for more information on this international reporting initiative. As shown, these include impacts to all three media – air, land and water. It is recommended that companies drawing up their own external cost accounts review the latest GRI *Guidelines* for help in identifying and assessing which impacts should be included within their accounts.

If the organisation has a registered environmental management system (EMS), the significant aspects register and/or other equivalent/related documentation prepared as part of the registration process is likely to list the majority of relevant issues to consider. Stakeholder dialogue carried out as part of the AA1000 process, for example, may also provide useful information. If no systems are in place, discussions with relevant company employees and common sense should provide sufficient information to get started.

Box 3: Overview of the Global Reporting Initiative (GRI)
Sustainability Reporting Guidelines

The Global Reporting Initiative (GRI) was established in late 1997 with the mission of developing globally-applicable guidelines for reporting on the economic, environmental and social performance, initially for corporations and eventually for any business, governmental or non-governmental organisation (NGO). Convened by the Coalition for Environmentally Responsible Economies (CERES) in partnership with the United Nations Environment Programme (UNEP), the GRI incorporates the active participation of corporations, NGOs, accountancy organisations, business associations and other stakeholders from around the world. The GRI's *Sustainability Reporting Guidelines* were released in exposure draft form in London in March 1999. The GRI Guidelines represent the first global framework for comprehensive sustainability reporting, encompassing the 'triple bottom line' of economic, environmental and social issues. Twenty-one pilot test companies, numerous other companies and a diverse array of non-corporate stakeholders commented on the draft *Guidelines* during a pilot test period in 1999-2000; revised *Guidelines* were released in June 2000. During 2002, the GRI will be established as a permanent, independent, international body with a multi-stakeholder governance structure. Its core mission will be maintenance, enhancement and dissemination of the *Guidelines* through a process of ongoing consultation and stakeholder engagement.

Source: *The GRI website – www.globalreporting.org*

4.4 Valuation of environmental impacts – avoidance and restoration costs

There are a number of environmental valuation techniques that can be used to obtain monetary valuations for environmental effects. This methodology aims to estimate what it would cost an individual organisation to deliver a given level of environmental improvement and to illustrate the impact of doing so on the company's bottom line. To facilitate this, impacts are valued, as far as possible, on the basis of what the individual company would need to spend in order to avoid the impacts in the first place or, if avoidance was not possible, on what it would need to spend to restore the resulting damage. No attempt is made to value the actual environmental effect or damage itself.[11] The objective is to identify and use 'real' or market-based prices for currently available technological solutions.

Box 4: The use of avoidance and restoration costs in the valuation of environmental effects

Abatement/avoidance costs: These refer to the actual costs of preventing environmental damage from taking place. They derive from measures that seek to reduce the pressures on environmental resources from current activities. For emissions, such measures may involve end-of-pipe abatement or substitutions in inputs, or process changes. For depletion, they may involve increasing the efficiency of resource use (which may also reduce emissions), increasing recycling, or substituting more for less abundant resources. The calculation of abatement/avoidance costs therefore depends on being able to calculate the costs of these abating or alternative technologies.

Restoration costs: While abatement/avoidance costs derive from measures to reduce environmental pressures, restoration costs relate to measures to improve environmental states. They may be required as a result of the environmental impacts of either current or past activities. For pollution they may be aimed at the improvement of the quality of air, water or land. For renewable resources, they may involve increasing the resource stock so that a higher annual harvest may be sustained. For non-renewable resources they may involve the development of technologies which make feasible the exploitation of inaccessible resources or those of a lower grade.

Damage costs: These refer to the value of the damage caused by the environmental effect. They comprise costs of environmental pollution and degradation and the opportunity costs of the depletion of environmental resources. While these costs may be the correct theoretical measure of environmental costs where it is desired to assess their welfare effects with a view to calculating environmental optimality, they are not per se related to environmental sustainability, which refers to the maintenance of environmental functions. High environmental damage costs may be an expressive indicator of environmental unsustainability. But, having determined the environmental improvement that is required for sustainability, the damage cost itself gives no insight into the economic implications of seeking to achieve this, which is required to value the sustainability gap. In addition, there are insuperable difficulties in measuring the damage costs of some of the most important environmental effects, e.g. those which involve major intergenerational effects, irreversibility, uncertainty or the loss of human life).

Source: Ekins, P and Simon S, (1998) Determining the Sustainability Gap: National Accounting For Environmental Sustainability, in *UK Environmental Accounts 1998*, eds P Vaze and JB Barron, The Stationery Office, London.

This approach is uncontroversial. However, establishing appropriate avoidance or restoration costs for all impacts, as discussed below, is not always straightforward and can be difficult. Box 4 provides further discussion on the various valuation techniques available. It should be noted that use of avoidance or restoration costs is in line with United Nations, recommendations for environmental adjustments to the national accounts.[12]

4.5 Individual cost line entries – estimation and worked examples

The remainder of Part 2 reviews each of the individual cost line entries in the pro-forma accounts to illustrate how organisations can go about the task of quantifying impacts and determining their own, company-relevant sustainability cost estimates. Source documents, conversion factors and illustrative valuations are also provided for most account headings together with a brief description of the nature of the impact under review. Please also refer to the relevant *Green Sheet* in Appendix 3 for further details and guidance. Box 6 (pp. 54–55) provides a more detailed overview of the environmental impacts associated with the main gaseous emissions that can be accounted for with this methodology.

5 Impacts to air

5.1 Direct energy use: electricity consumption

- **Key impacts:** associated with emissions of carbon dioxide from the use of fossil fuels consumed in the generation of the electricity, also acidification from emissions of sulphur dioxide and impacts resulting from the formation of photochemical smog from emissions of nitrogen oxides.
- **Data source:** utility bills, meter readings.
- **Conversion factors:** CO_2 DETR guidelines for company reporting on greenhouse emissions (DETR/DEFRA guidelines) gives 0.44 g/kWh; NOx 0.0012g/kWh (UK Digest of energy statistics); SOx 0.0025g/kWh (UK Digest of energy statistics).
- **Valuation:** Emissions associated with the consumption of grid electricity can largely be avoided by purchasing electricity generated from renewable energy sources, such as wind power.[13] An illustrative

valuation to use would be any premium payable on purchasing 'green electricity'. Some companies (those with relatively low total demand) have achieved the switch at no extra premium. Consequently, to determine a company-relevant avoidance cost for energy-related emissions, it is recommended that contact is made with the company's current electricity supplier and one or two of the providers of renewable electricity such as Unit E and Eco-tricity. Any premiums payable to secure 'green' electricity will – in part – be determined by the individual company's demand and load profile.

Other valuations could include the costs associated with on-site power generation from renewable energy sources. Both AWG and Wessex are exploring the development of on-site renewable generation – wind and Combined Heat and Power (CHP) – and the costs associated with these development plus company specific premiums to purchase a proportion of total supplies from renewable tariffs were used to determine this component of their direct energy, use sustainability, cost estimations.

Many of the companies using this methodology have used a 'default' avoidance cost of 3p/kWh for valuing their electricity-related emissions (generally applying this premium to 60 per cent (their sustainability target) of their total electricity consumption). This is based on what the electricity suppliers will have to pay the Government for any shortfall they have in meeting their obligation to ensure that 10 per cent of total electricity supplies are generated from renewable energy sources by 2010 (a UK Government policy target). The Renewables Obligation, to ensure this target is met, now places a statutory obligation on the electricity suppliers (from April 2002) to hold Renewable Obligation Certificates (ROCs) which represent the appropriate level of purchased renewable energy under the Obligation (building to 10 per cent by 2010). ROCs are already trading for about £30/MW (i.e. 3p/kWh) which suggests this price is a reasonable avoidance cost to use. Use can also be made of the illustrative 'generic' valuations shown below. Companies should aim to use the most appropriate and company-relevant valuation options available to them.

- **Carbon dioxide**
  £5.45/tonne of carbon dioxide – avoidance/restoration cost based on market price currently being charged by Climate Care. Climate Care invests in renewable energy technologies, energy efficiency and carbon sequestration through the planting of new woodlands.

- **Nitrogen oxides**
  £14,000/tonne (based on the top end of recent NOx trading prices in the USA and rates used in other similar studies).
- **Sulphur dioxide**
  £2,400 (based on recent EU and Scandinavian environmental tax rates).

5.2 Direct energy use: gas consumption

- **Key impacts:** associated with emissions of carbon dioxide from gas consumption. Emissions of other gaseous emissions are unlikely to be significant/material.
- **Data source:** utility bills, meter readings.
- **Conversion factors:** DETR guidelines for company reporting on greenhouse emissions (DETR guidelines) gives 0.19kg/CO_2 per kWh.
- **Valuation Carbon dioxide** £5.45/tonne (Climate Care avoidance/ restoration market price as above).

Example

For an annual consumption of 9 million kWhs, the relevant figure (avoidance/restoration cost in this case) to include in the accounts would be £9,000 (to the nearest thousand) – i.e. 9 million*0.19*£5.45.

As noted in the Green Sheets in Appendix 3 (table 1), other potential sources of direct, energy-related emissions could include consumption of propane and fuel oil. This list is by no means exhaustive.

6 Direct production-related emissions

This heading is likely only to apply to manufacturing companies. Impacts will obviously vary considerably depending upon the nature of the organisation. For example, Interface Europe, one of the companies using this methodology, has a number of direct gaseous emissions – including emissions of volatile organic compounds (VOCs) and sulphur dioxide (SO_2) – associated with their production processes.

To comply with current legislation, emission levels have to be measured periodically; consequently the company already had quantified emission data. The valuation of these emissions were determined by obtaining quotations from environmental technology companies for the retro-fitting of pollution abatement technology to reduce these emissions by between 60–100 per cent (the chosen sustainability targets for these particular emissions). This capital cost provided a real, market-based price for the avoidance of the majority of the emissions. Depending upon the significance of any capital costs of this nature, it may be necessary to capitalise the investment and to charge depreciation to the external cost accounts according to the company's depreciation policy.

7 Transportation

7.1 Company cars

- **Key impacts:** gaseous emissions including volatile organic compounds (VOCs), hydrocarbons (HC), particular matter (PM) and carbon dioxide (CO_2). Transport-related emissions linked to asthma, respiratory disease, premature deaths, cancer, etc. (not to mention general poor urban air quality, congestion and loss of habitat).
- **Data source:** transport managers, fixed asset registers to get full listing of all vehicles – numbers and make and engine size, fuel type, etc . and direct from leasing companies where applicable.
- **Conversion factors:** these can vary enormously depending upon the age, make, fuel type and size of the vehicle. New vehicles have considerably lower emission coefficients. An excellent information source on emissions by make and model is provided by the Government's (DETR's) Cleaner Vehicle Task Force. For example, see its publication *New Car Fuel Consumption and Emission Figures*. Emission data is also available from the EU, OECD, AEA Technology and others. Illustrative emission co-efficients for a popular company car, the Ford Focus 1.6 are shown below:

Emission levels for a new (meeting Euro II) popular company car

Ford Focus 1.6	g/km	Illustrative valuation
CO_2	153	£5.45/tonne (Climate Care sequestration (restoration) cost)
HC and NOx	0.097	Avoidance cost – LPG conversion (see below)

It may be easier and more practical to estimate total emissions by class of vehicle, i.e. all petrol vehicles of a certain size range, all diesel vehicles of a certain size, etc. If accurate fuel consumption data is available, more accurate estimates for carbon dioxide emissions can be obtained by following the DETR greenhouse gas reporting guidelines.

An excellent source of information on emissions from mobile and point source can be found at the DEFRA's (formally the DETR's) UK Emission Factors Database web site: www.rsk.co.uk/ukefd/

- **Valuation:** Apart from driving less miles (e.g. by avoiding unnecessary journeys and making greater use of public transport) and to a limited degree, driving the same miles but at lower speeds, there are not many options to reduce total emissions of gaseous pollutants from modern (less than three years old) petrol or diesel-fuelled vehicles. Emissions from these vehicles have been reduced by an order of magnitude (per vehicle mile) compared to a decade ago.

Ultimately, hydrogen fuel cells, which have the potential to emit only warm water vapour, offer the prospect of avoiding harmful vehicle emissions almost entirely (during the use phase of a vehicle's lifetime at least). However, the widespread commercial availability of such vehicles still remains some time off, despite the development of a number of prototypes. In the meantime, however, there are a number of 'technical fix' interim or partial solutions that can be used to help to reduce overall transport-related emissions. One involves the use of alternative 'clean' fuels such as Liquid Petroleum Gas (LPG) and Compressed Natural Gas (CNG). Whilst emissions of carbon dioxide remain similar to those of conventional petrol and diesel vehicles, emissions of PM, VOCs, and NOx are substantially reduced. Compared to petrol engines, for example, oxides of nitrogen are reduced by some 50 per cent and hydrocarbons by between 40-95 per cent with LPG vehicles.

Consequently, a significant proportion of transport-related emissions (excluding carbon dioxide) could be avoided by either purchasing or leasing LPG vehicles or perhaps by switching to compressed natural gas. Grants may also be available through the Powershift Programme, administered by the Energy Savings Trust (EST), for converting existing vehicles to run off LPG or to contribute to the purchase of factory-produced LPG vehicles. Given the difference in fuel costs – LPG is typically available for as little as 25p/litre for bunker fuel or around 40p/litre at the forecourt compared to 80p/litre for diesel – the business case for making the switch is already very strong, irrespective of any environmental arguments.[14]

A typical conversion cost may be around £1,500 per vehicle – this could be an appropriate valuation to use for petrol vehicles and represents an appropriate avoidance cost for the majority of harmful, non-carbon dioxide emissions associated with petrol vehicles. The cost should be shown gross of any grants that may be available, although the grants will clearly be an important consideration in the decision-making process.

Other technological options may be available to reduce emissions and hence the cost of the relevant technology would be an appropriate valuation to use in the accounts. For example, oxidation catalysts can be retro-fitted to older and larger diesel vehicles. Alternatively, the cost of trading in existing vehicles and purchasing new hybrid vehicles such as the Toyota Prius could be used as the basis of valuation. Consideration could also be given to the accelerated depreciation and write-off of older vehicles and their replacement with more fuel-efficient and cleaner vehicles. Any premiums payable on the early termination of current leases or additional costs associated with the earlier purchase of new vehicles would then provide an appropriate valuation/cost to include in the accounts for the emissions avoided by adopting such a policy. If alternative fuel/dual fuel vehicles are purchased, there may actually be a net saving from such a policy.

7.2 Haulage/distribution

Similarly, significant emission reductions of hydrocarbons and particulate matter from large diesel vehicles can be achieved through the retro-fitting of existing vehicles with Continuously Regenerating Traps (CRTs). These catalysts, produced by Johnson Matthey, are capable of reducing emissions of hydrocarbons and particulate matter from exhaust fumes by 90 per cent.[15] Retro-fits cost in the region of about £3000 per vehicle.

Other options, as noted above, could include the premium to purchase new, more fuel-efficient and lower impact vehicles over any trade in value resulting from the accelerated depreciation of existing vehicles. If avoidance options are not available/appropriate, carbon dioxide emissions should be valued on the basis of their restoration costs – as noted an illustrative figure of £5.45/tonne from Climate Care can be used (generally rounded up to £6/tonne in the accounts). Nitrogen oxide emissions (often reported/aggregated with hydrocarbon emissions) can be valued at the illustrative cost of £14,000/tonne. This figure is very high and where gaseous emissions are aggregated, is likely to overstate the sustainability cost estimate, hence, wherever possible, more appropriate avoidance or restoration costs should be used. As noted above, the illustrative £14,000/tonne cost factor is based on the upper end of recent trading prices under one of the US NOx emissions trading systems. Trading prices, at least in theory, reflect the marginal cost of abatement of the emissions being traded.

7.3 Third party carriers

Given that many organisations contract their deliveries and freight movements to third party carriers, it is important to ensure that accurate estimates of contractor mileage, fuel consumption, etc. by type and size of vehicle are obtained to ensure that the impacts associated with this activity are captured. For many of the companies engaged in external cost accounting, this source of transport-related emissions have accounted for 50 per cent or more of gaseous emissions to air. Consequently, their exclusion from the accounts could result in transport-related impacts being significantly understated. Obtaining detailed information on third party carriers/contractor mileage can also provide a useful starting point for supply chain management – setting targets to reduce contractor mileage and impacts and developing new ways to share the benefits down the supply chain of any cost savings achieved.

7.4 Aviation

Aviation is responsible for a myriad of external environmental impacts including significant (and increasing) emissions of gaseous pollutants (from aircraft and ground operations), congestion, loss of biodiversity through the building of airport infrastructure, contamination of land and ground water, and so on. To date, the companies using this methodology have only accounted for the emissions of carbon dioxide and nitrogen oxides associated with aircraft fuel burn, i.e. the direct, marginal environmental costs/impacts resulting from their employees' use of air travel. This clearly understates the true or full external costs associated with air travel and it is hoped that further development and refinement of the methodology will enable some of these wider impacts, where appropriate (depending upon the choice of system boundaries adopted) to be included.

Total emissions of these gases can be determined from total air miles by applying the following conversion factors:

LTO emissions (landing and take off)
- Carbon dioxide   35,000 g/passenger

Cruising emissions
- Carbon dioxide   184 g/passenger km
- Nitrogen oxides   0.432 g/passenger km

Air mile data should be available from the company travel agent. All companies involved in the development of this methodology have required, or are in the process of requiring, their travel agents to provide this information. Alternatively, with a schedule of points of departure and arrival and number of flights flown on that route, an approximation of total air miles can be found via various internet sites, for example, *How far is it?* The RAC have a useful site that can be used to estimate land-based journeys by road and rail.[16]

8 Impacts to land

8.1 Disposal of waste to landfill

Waste is a major sustainability challenge. It has been estimated that the UK generates between 170 million and 210 million tonnes of waste each year. Nearly 60 per cent of this waste is disposed of to a diminishing number of UK landfill sites. By sector, around 55 per cent of commercial and industrial waste and 82 per cent of municipal waste is disposed of via this route. As noted early, the linear nature of our production and consumption systems that create this enormous volume of waste each year are inherently unsustainable. We simply cannot carry on indefinitely, on a finite planet, taking stuff out of the ground, processing and/or manufacturing it only for it to be used, perhaps just once, before throwing it away. It is costly in more ways than one, represents an inefficient use of resources and is now beginning to overwhelm us as we run out of holes in the ground to bury it.

The main environmental impacts attributable to waste disposal to landfill are as follows:

- emissions of greenhouse gases (methane and carbon dioxide from the landfill sites themselves);
- leaching of contaminated and, in some instances, toxic chemicals into water bodies (with associated impacts on the chemical and biological oxygen demand for the receiving watercourses);
- contamination of the landfill site itself;
- impacts on habitat and biodiversity from the construction and operation of landfill sites;
- congestion and emissions of air pollutants from the transportation of waste.

EU waste legislation, for example the Waste Framework Directive and its so-called 'Daughter Directives' – the Landfill Directive in particular – will require Member States to move waste management up the so-called waste hierarchy. This will mean decreasing the volumes of waste disposed of to landfill and incineration, which are at the bottom of the hierarchy, and increasing the volume of materials recovered and re-used. This will impact on UK companies – the way they manage their waste, how much they pay for its disposal and the availability of alternative disposal (and avoidance) routes open to them.[17] Ideally, waste generation should be avoided in the first place – through the design of new products and processes and from careful materials selection.

UK businesses are already paying for some of the external costs of waste disposal through the landfill tax, either directly or indirectly via the charges they pay to their waste disposal contractors. The tax was introduced in October 1996 at rates based on estimations of the external costs of waste disposal commissioned by the then Department of the Environment (DoE) (CSERGE *et al.*, 1993). The initial rates payable when the tax was introduced were £10 per tonne for active waste and £2 per tonne for inert waste. It could therefore be argued, perhaps, that waste disposal to landfill should be excluded from the external cost accounts. Companies have already internalised these costs. However, despite the announcement in the 1999 Budget that the standard tax rate would increase by £1 per year until 2004 it is unlikely that the tax does or will, if capped at £15/tonne in 2004, capture all of the external costs attributable to waste disposal.

Consequently, companies should provide an additional amount per tonne of waste disposed of to landfill to cover these additional and 'unaccounted for' external costs. Whilst there is uncertainty over what the true or full external costs of waste disposal may be, the use of an £18 per tonne premium is now being used by several companies engaged in the use of this methodology. This premium seems reasonable. It is based on the differential between the current UK tax rates and the most progressive landfill tax rate in continental Europe – the Austrian landfill. The Austrian tax, currently charged at £28/tonne, is designed to offer incentives to reduce the level of waste disposed of in landfills and to generate additional revenues to support the cleaning up of contaminated sites as well as encouraging the transition towards sites with 'state of the art' technology. It could therefore be considered as the nearest thing we have to a 'restoration cost' for waste disposal at this time.

8.2 Contaminated land

Centuries of industrial activity in the UK have left the country with an unquantified, but significant, stock of contaminated land – land contaminated with a range of chemical and often persistent pollutants. These include toxic metals, such as lead, arsenic and mercury from mines, iron and steel works and the electroplating industry, flammable gases and corrosive leachates from landfills, and a vast array of substances from chemical works, refineries and waste disposal sites.

There is a great deal of uncertainty over the true extent of the problem in the UK. Estimates suggest that somewhere in the region of 100,000–200,000 hectares of land may be chemically contaminated. This area may cover some 100,000–150,000 sites. The potential health impacts, risks and economic costs associated with such contamination are well illustrated by the Love Canal incident in the USA and a similar incident at Lekkerkerk, in the Netherlands. In both cases, residential houses had been built on land previously contaminated by toxic chemical wastes. Residents became ill, drinking water was contaminated and contaminated leachates were found in cellars and building voids. The Love Canal site was eventually declared a national emergency and both sites required multi-million dollar clean up programmes.[18]

Financial liability is at the heart of the contaminated land debate. Dealing with contaminated sites will impose costs on both the public and private sectors. Some estimates suggest that around £500 million per year is already being spent on dealing with contamination in England and Wales alone. Other estimates suggest that the total clean up costs of all contaminated sites could eventually be in the region of £10 billion to £30 billion.

Consequently, the presence of contaminated land is likely to be an issue for many organisations, especially where industrial activity has taken place on the site over several decades. Site investigations should be able to provide a suitable valuation for inclusion in the accounts, i.e. in effect, a restoration cost for the environmental damage caused. Whilst it may seem unfair to provide for the full costs of restoration in one year, since any damage that may have occurred could have taken place over several decades, it is probably prudent to do so. In many cases, where material, the likely clean up and restoration costs of any contaminated sites identified, as a contingent liability, will require a provision in the main financial accounts – irrespective of whether or not the company decides to provide for their other identified external environmental costs. See section 10 on *Providing for the Restoration of Natural Capital* for more discussion on the accounting treatment of a company's quantified external/sustainability costs.

9 Impacts to water

The UK water industry supplies over 19,500 million litres of water per day to about 60 million people. At least 20,000 million litres of sewage arrives daily at sewage treatment plants, resulting in the production of over 1 million dry tonnes of sewage sludge annually.

The main sustainability challenges relating to water use are the underlying sustainability of supply of the resource itself and also the significant and growing emissions of greenhouse gases associated with the energy-intensive treatment of waste water. Billions of pounds have been spent by the privatised water companies since 1989 to deliver higher water quality standards – both inland river water quality and coastal bathing water quality – and we are now reaching the point where the benefits of higher standards may no longer be outweighed by the marginal costs, environmental and financial, of achieving them.

For the water companies themselves, another key sustainability challenge relates to the issue of abstraction (a supply issue) at vulnerable sites. Overabstraction from low-flow rivers, for example, at times of drought can result in significant environmental damage and stress to the areas affected. In some instances rivers have ceased flowing altogether. As shown in Wessex Water's External Environmental Cost Accounts (see Figure 5), the provision of alternative supplies at priority 'vulnerable' sites was the largest single cost line entry in the company's accounts.

External impacts to water have not been found to be significant for the non-manufacturing companies using this methodology. It could be argued that companies internalise many of the external costs associated with their use of water through the water rates and charges they pay to their local water company. However, as for the landfill tax, it is unlikely that current water charges capture the full external costs associated with water supply and consumption. These costs (those actually paid and the full external costs) are also likely to increase as the impacts of global climate change, particularly in relation to supply in drought-prone parts of the country such as East Anglia, become more apparent.

Two of the manufacturing companies using this methodology – Interface Europe and Bulmers – have found that on-site investment in waste water treatment and/or modifications to production processes to improve the quality of their waste water effluent (both its Biological Oxygen Demand (BOD) and Chemical Oxygen Demand (COD)) can lead to substantial financial savings as well as decreasing their external environmental impacts. These investments effectively internalise the external costs of their waste water discharges and provide appropriate avoidance costs to use in their external cost accounts. For example, Interface made simple modifications to its carpet dyeing processes and installed a waste water treatment tank to ensure that the ph of their trade effluent matched that of the receiving watercourse. These investments paid back for themselves in less than one year. Bulmers, the Herefordshire-based cider manufacturer, is currently exploring the development of a 'living system' – a series of ponds with different plants and aquatic ecosystems, that will dramatically reduce the BOD of their trade effluent from the apple mill. This 'living system' could save hundreds of thousands of pounds in trade effluent charges and reduce the external environmental impacts of their waste water discharges considerably.

It is hoped that further development of this methodology will identify appropriate 'generic' valuations/costs to be applied to both water use (litres supplied) and waste water discharges (litres discharged) to enable companies to include and internalise this component of their external cost within their environmental accounts. Factors may also need to be determined for companies'/organisations' (particularly farming and manufacturing businesses) use of on-site abstraction/borehole water. For now, it is recommended that companies quantify their water consumption and discharges, review their water charges and, at the very least, disclose their consumption figures within their external cost accounts. Manufacturing companies should also explore the avoidance opportunities available to them to reduce costs and impacts as outlined above.

Box 5: Accounting for the environment – the experience of BSO Origin and Landcare Research (New Zealand) Ltd

BSO Origin

In 1990, BSO Origin, a Dutch management consultancy company, produced an innovative set of environmental accounts. The accounts attempted to quantify in financial terms, the value extracted by the company but not paid for. BSO Origin continued to produce environmental accounts for several years until the company was eventually sold to a large Anglo-Dutch multinational. In their 1990 accounts, the net value lost (or 'cost of environmental effects') is deducted from the conventional economic value added by the company to produce a net value added. The methodology detailed in this guide has drawn on the pioneering work undertaken by BSO Origin. However, there are several differences in the approaches adopted by the two studies: the most important concerns the approach to environmental valuation. In their 1995 report, BSO state that its preferred approach to valuing environmental impacts is to make use of actual damage cost estimates. This is in sharp contrast to the approach outlined in the main report. BSO also makes use of prevention and restoration costs. Consequently, the numbers are not comparable. As Rob Gray notes, BSO 'add possible apples to approximate pears and subtract the result from hypothetical oranges'. (see Gray et. al. (1993)). By focusing on avoidance and restoration costs based on actual market prices the methodology discussed in this guide hopes to avoid this problem. In addition, when arriving at an estimate for what could be considered as a company's environmentally-sustainable profits, Forum's approach applies the concept of limits or sustainability standards. Internalising external damage costs could still result in a level of activity that was unsustainable.

Landcare Research (New Zealand) Ltd – (Manaaki Whenua)

Landcare Research is a Crown Research Institute that conducts research into the sustainable management of land eco-systems, including their productive uses and conservation of natural resources. The Landcare project, undertaken by Professor Jan Bebbington, also drew on the pioneering work undertaken by BSO Origin. However, in common with Forum's methodology it attempted to apply the idea of the sustainability cost calculation to an individual organisation. It was the first such practical experiment of this kind. The method used in the project involved modelling a series of incremental cost steps the organisation would have to go through in order to move towards sustainability. The financial quantification of an organisation's impacts was separated into two parts:

1. related to the incremental costs associated with purchasing from more sustainable sources.

2. related to the cost of remedying of the environmental effects arising from the organisation's activities, including past damage.

However, no options for purchasing goods and services from more sustainable sources were found and the financial quantification of impacts was limited to some cost estimates relating to carbon emissions only. The authors concluded that the clean-up costs associated with emissions, except for carbon, could not be estimated. This was due to the uncertainty that surrounded the way the emissions interact and on how to remedy their effect. Unlike the work undertaken by Interface, AWG and the other companies discussed in this guide, no attempt was made to link the organisations environmental performance data to the company's financial accounting information – i.e. to estimate Landcare's environmentally-sustainable or environmentally-adjusted profits.

For a more detailed discussion on the Landcare Project see Bebbington, J and Gray, R, *An Account of Sustainability: Failure, Success and a Reconceptualization*, *Critical Perspectives on Accounting*, (2001), vol 12, pp. 557–587.

Box 6: The environmental impacts associated with the main gaseous emissions resulting from manufacturing enterprises

Carbon dioxide (CO_2)

The two main sources of anthroprogenic emissions of carbon dioxide are fossil fuel combustion and deforestation (cement production is also important). Together with emissions of methane (largely from agriculture), nitrous oxide (N_2O from agriculture and industry) and other man-made greenhouse gases such as (hydroflurocarbons (HFCs), perflurocarbons (PFCs) and sulphur hexafluoride (SF_6) carbon dioxide emissions are enhancing the earth's natural greenhouse effect. Carbon dioxide emissions alone are responsible for some 64% of this total human enhanced (global) warming. The enhanced greenhouse effect is expected to alter atmospheric and oceanic temperatures and associated circulatory and weather patterns. The frequency and intensity of extreme weather events are expected to increase and sea levels are predicted to rise by half a metre by 2100. Evidence of global climate change may already be here. Ice sheets are melting, sea levels are rising and the cost of storm-related damage, an indicator of a warmer and more turbulent climate, have increased six-fold this decade. In the UK, 1998 was the hottest year since records began and seven of the warmest have occurred in the 1990s and 16 of the hottest since 1980.

Volatile Organic Compounds (VOCs)

Volatile Organic Compounds (VOCs) emissions result from the use of hydrocarbons in almost every aspect of the production, use and disposal of commercial, domestic and personal products. Major sources include emissions resulting from the use of solvents (in painting, printing, metal cleaning and personal products), road transport (combustion of fuels, evaporation of petrol, etc.), the chemical industry and stationary combustion (power stations, waste incineration and agriculture). Anthroprogenic VOC emissions are currently estimated to be in the order of 10 million tonnes a year in Europe. UK emissions total some 2.4 million tonnes. VOCs are a major contributor to poor and declining standards of urban air quality. The main pollution issue surrounding VOC emissions concerns their role in the formation of photochemical oxidants such as tropospheric ozone which are toxic to humans, damage ecosystems and exacerbate the problem of acid rain. These are formed when VOCs react with oxides of nitrogen (NOx) (see below) in the presence of sunlight.

Nitrogen oxides (NOx) and particulate matter (PM)

Nitrogen oxides, together with hydrocarbons and VOC emissions, are precursors of photochemical smog. The main sources are road transport, accounting for over 50% of total emissions, and industry. Road transport is also responsible for nearly 50% of particulate emissions. There is increasing evidence of the link between exposure to these and other air pollutants and adverse effects in human health. In 1994 *New Scientist* reported the findings of a study that suggested that airborne particulate matter levels in England and Wales may account for 24,000 deaths annually. Other studies have shown associations between respiratory disease and SO_2 and smoke at levels well below current European guide values. The dramatic increase in asthma has also been linked to rising emissions from vehicles. Recorded asthma cases in the UK increased by 136% between 1979 and 1990 and one in seven children is now reported to suffer from asthma.

Sulphur dioxide (SO_2)

Sulphur dioxide is one of the two principal pollutants responsible for the formation of acid rain (the other being nitrogen oxides). The major source of SO_2 emissions is the electricity supply industry, which accounts for about 70% of total UK emissions; industry is responsible for the bulk of the remainder. Damage resulting from acid rain includes the acidification of lakes and streams (which in severe cases results in the appearance of dead 'lakes', forest dieback, loss of agricultural production, and damage to human health (mainly aggravating respiratory problems). Acid rain is also responsible for damaging masonry, paint and other building materials.

Source: Howes, R, Skea, J and Whelan, B, (1997), *Clean and Competitive: Motivating Environmental Performance in Industry*, Earthscan, London.

55

10   Providing for the restoration of natural capital

The sustainability cost estimate represents what it would have cost the company to avoid or restore the most significant external environmental impacts resulting from its activities and operations over the accounting period under review. This estimate needs to be deducted from the company's financial profit or loss account as reported to obtain a measure of what could be considered, given the caveats already discussed above, as the company's environmentally-sustainable or adjusted profits. In an ideal world, the sustainability cost estimate should be provided in full in the company's main accounts and the provision used over subsequent periods to make the sustainability investments required to reduce the organisation's external environmental footprint. Forum for the Future produces its own external cost accounts and although the sums involved are not large, provides for the estimated sustainability cost each year – i.e. internalises the costs within the organisation's mainstream financial accounts (the accounts can be seen on Forum's web page – www.forumforthefuture.org.uk). After three years of producing external cost accounts a cumulative provision of about £13,000 has been made. This provision is now being used to fund the switch to green electricity tariffs at all of the organisation's main offices and also to fund the planting and maintenance of a new mixed deciduous woodland. In addition to creating new habitat and enhancing biodiversity, the woodland will also contribute to offsetting some of Forum's carbon dioxide emissions.

To date, AWG, Wessex Water, Marks and Spencer, Interface and Bulmers have decided not to provide formally for their sustainability cost estimates in their main financial accounts. This may just be a step too far at this stage and perhaps harder to justify to a demanding City when their cost estimates have been between 8 per cent and 10 per cent of their post-tax profits on ordinary activities (for the UK companies). They are, however, all making the sorts of sustainability investments identified through their engagement in environmental accounting that will help them to reduce their cost estimates over future years – i.e. they are beginning to internalise these costs with or without an appropriate/relevant provision. One of these companies also hopes to be in a position where it can provide for its sustainability cost estimate in full within a period of perhaps five years or so from now. To achieve this the company in question has already embarked upon a process of raising awareness amongst its existing shareholders and other external financial stakeholders of the importance of becoming a sustainable enterprise, and the business case and benefits of doing so.

Environmental accounting is a process and it takes time to embed it within an organisation and to win the hearts and minds of key decision-makers. There can be obstacles and barriers to overcome but all of these companies are committed to the continued use and development of environmental accounting and, in most cases, public reporting. Environmental accounting is seen to add value, have the potential to help to reduce and manage business risk and without doubt, provide a means to communicate an organisation's positive and proactive approach to environmental management and sustainability (whether internally or externally) and hence to differentiate itself from its competitors. It also provides a powerful change management, awareness raising and transformation tool that can, over time, contribute to making environmental and sustainability thinking part of the mainstream of an organisation's culture and operations.

11 Conclusions

External cost accounting is still evolving. Consequently the accounting framework described in this introductory guide is likely to undergo some changes as more companies begin to engage and experiment with the methodology. It has, after all, taken us several centuries to develop the current, and still dynamic, framework of financial accounting and reporting standards. However, the broad approach is likely to remain constant – namely, to identify where a company is in terms of its environmental impacts, to determine appropriate 'sustainability' targets or standards to aim for, and to work out the most cost-effective way for the company to close that 'sustainability gap.' Greater understanding of environmental sustainability and improvements in scientific understanding will lead to more appropriate and generally higher targets being set. In any event, it seems likely that, as Bulmers Group Financial Manager, Dave Marshall, noted in a recent article, eventually every company will have to make these calculations as part of routine accounting and reporting requirements, particularly as investors begin to ask questions about the cost of unsustainable business. As Marshall commented, 'there is something to be said for being prepared, for anticipating these concerns and getting systems in place at an early stage.' [19]

For more information please contact:

Rupert Howes
Director – Sustainable Economy Programme
Forum for the Future
Tel. 020 7324 3610
Email *r.howes@forumforthefuture.org.uk*

Footnotes

[6] – See section 4.1 below for a discussion on the implications of drawing narrow system boundaries and how the methodology can be, and is already being, extended to include the wider life-cycle impacts associated with the manufacture, use and final disposal of products at the end of their useful lives.

[7] – The sustainability cost approach is one of three ways identified by Rob Gray and Jan Bebbington to enable organisations to begin to account for sustainability (Gray et al., 1993). Forum's external cost accounting work draws on this concept in developing a methodology that could be employed by companies to account for the external environmental impacts resulting from their activities. It also draws on the pioneering work on environmental accounting undertaken by BSO Origin, the Dutch management consultancy company.

[8] – Offsetting incentives, grants and savings associated with the individual cost line entries detailed in Anglian Water Service's environmental accounts (over all three periods) were estimated to be in the region of several million pounds. These savings are not shown in the financial highlights. The main items, under current institutional and legislative arrangements, include exemptions from the climate change levy, offsetting grants under the Government's Powershift Programme (towards the costs of converting vehicles to run off alternative fuels), vehicle licence rebates and significant reductions in AWS's total road fuel bills.

[9] – Environmental Reporting: Guidelines for company reporting on greenhouse gas emissions, DETR, June 1999, London.

[10] – A product's or service's life-cycle impacts would include all of the external impacts associated with its manufacture, use and final disposal – i.e. it would include the upstream impacts associated with the production and distribution of raw material and other inputs into the organisation's own production process and the downstream impacts resulting from the use and final

disposal of the goods at the end of their useful lives. For example, in relation to motor vehicles, upstream impacts would include those resulting from the extraction of primary ores, their mining, transportation and processing into steel and aluminium sheet for a car's basic frame, the carbon dioxide and other gaseous emissions emitted from road vehicles during use, and the costs and impacts associated with the final disposal of the vehicle at the end of its useful life.

11 – There is no necessary relationship between damage, restoration and avoidance costs. However, where that damage has been inflicted on an economic asset – i.e. the damage is clearly visible – restoration and damage costs can be equal. Where the damage is done to an ecosystem this connection is lost.

12 – The United Nations Statistical Division's Handbook on Integrated Environmental and Economic Accounting (UN 1993).

13 – Most electricity generated from renewable energy sources results in no net additional carbon loading of the atmosphere. In fact, by displacing supplies generated from fossil fuels, renewable sources actually help to reduce overall carbon emissions. Emissions of SO_2 and NOx from electricity generated from renewable sources will vary depending upon the renewable energy source being used to generate the electricity. If the supply has been generated from wind, hydro or photovoltaics (i.e. so called 'new renewables') there are no gaseous emissions (ignoring life-cycle impacts). In contrast, the combustion of biomass, sewage gas or landfill gas will result in emissions of NOx and some SO_2 (because of impurities in the gas). For simplicity, the figures reflected in the environmental accounts shown in this guide have assumed that conventionally-generated supplies have been switched for supplies generated entirely from wind power. Consequently, it has been assumed that all gaseous emissions associated with electricity production have been avoided.

14 – Based on summer 2002 fuel prices.

15 – Emissions of nitrogen oxides are only reduced by a maximum of 12%. The CRT is primarily designed to remove soot, and at this time, there are no readily available technical fixes that can be retrofitted to reduce these NOx emissions.

16 – How far is it? can be found at: www.indo.com/distance/index.html and RAC European Route Planner can be found at: www.route2.rac.co.uk/webroute212/names.asp

[17] – As noted in the DETR Environmental Reporting Guidelines for Company Reporting on Waste, most companies should already be aware of the wastes they produce and where they go. The Environment Protection Act 1990 places a Duty of Care on anyone who produces commercial or industrial waste. This means that all companies must secure their waste and can only transfer it to an authorised person with a transfer note. This implies waste records and recording should be good, or of a standard, even if this data is not being publicly reported. With the Packaging Regulations, Landfill Directive and likelihood of further legislation around the areas of Producer Responsibility and Integrated Product Policy companies are going to have to develop comprehensive strategies and policies for managing and reducing all of their waste flows. They will have no choice in the matter, and the DETR/DEFRA Guidelines have been produced to help them achieve this.

[18] – Between 1942 and 1952, the Hooker Electrochemical Company dumped 210,000 tonnes of chemical waste, including caustic substances, alkalis and solvents into the Love Canal in Upper New York State. The dump was sealed with a layer of clay and subsequently used as the site of a school and housing estate. By the mid-1970s the waste containers had begun to corrode and a series of heavy rains washed the chemicals into underground waterways and thence into gardens and cellars. In 1976 chemical contamination from Love Canal was detected in Lake Ontario and in 1980 over 700 families were evacuated. In addition to personal claims, Hooker faced a claim of $125 million from the US Environmental Protection Agency. Clean-up work on the site cost a further $1.3 billion.

[19] – Cowe, R, (March–April 2001), In the black, red or green, Green Futures, Issue 27, pp. 60–61, Forum for the Future, London.

References and
further information

Selected references and other sources of information

'Accounting for the Environment – Leading Companies are now beginning to experiment with innovative environmental accounting methodologies to 'take nature into account', in *Environmental Accountant and Auditing Reporter*, September 2000, pp. 5–7, ACCA, London.

'Accounting for Environmentally Sustainable Profits', in *Management Accounting*, Vol. 77, No. 1, January 1999, (pp. 32–33), Chartered Institute of Management Accounting (CIMA), London.

Advances in Environmental Accounting. Proceedings of the ACCA/Environment Agency Seminar May 2001, Certified Accountants Educational Trust, London, 2001.

Advisory Committee on Business and the Environment (ACBE), February (1997) Report, *Environmental Reporting and the Financial Sector: An approach to Good Practice,* DoE, London.

Bennett, M and James, P (1998) eds. *The Green Bottom Line: Environmental Accounting for Management Current Practice and Future Trends,* Greenleaf Publishing, Sheffield.

Bennett, M and James, P (1999) eds, *Sustainable Measures – Evaluation and Reporting of Environmental and Social Performance,* Greenleaf Publishing, Sheffield.

Bebbington, J et al., (2001) *Full Cost Accounting: An Agenda for Action*, ACCA Research Report No. 73. Certified Accountants Educational Trust, London.

Bebbington, J and Gray, R (2001), 'An Account of Sustainability: Failure, Success and a Reconceptualization', *Critical Perspectives on Accounting*, vol.12, pp. 557–587

Bebbington J. and Tan, J. 'Accounting for Sustainability', *Chartered Accountants Journal.* July 1996 & February 1997.

BT Environmental Issues Unit (1996), *Environmental Accounting in Industry: A Practical Review*, London.

Cowe, R, (March–April 2001), *In the black, red or green,* Green Futures, Issue 27, pp. 60–61, Forum for the Future, London.

Daryl, D et al. (1995), *Green Ledgers: Case Studies in Corporate Environmental Accounting,* World Resource Institute (WRI), New York, USA.

Daryl, D and Ranganathan, J (1997), *Measuring Up: Toward a Common Framework for Tracking Corporate Environmental Performance*, World Resource Institute (WRI), New York, USA.

Ditz, D, Ranganathan, R and Darryl Banks, R (1995), *Green Ledgers,* World Resources Institute, Washington, DC.

Ekins, P (2000), *Economic Growth and Environmental Sustainability – The Prospects for Green Growth*, Routledge, London.

Ekins, P and Simon, S (1998), 'Determining the Sustainability Gap: National Accounting For Environmental Sustainability'. Chapter 9 in *UK Environmental Accounts 1998*, eds. Vaze, P and Barron, JB, The Stationery Office, London.

Gray, R et al. (1993), *Accounting for the Environment*, Paul Chapman Publishing, London.

Howes, R (2000), Corporate Environmental Accounting: Accounting for Environmentally Sustainable Profits, in *Greening the Accounts,* eds. J Proops and S Simon, A Volume in the *Current Issues in Ecological Economics*, Edward Elgar Publishers, UK.

Howes, R, Skea, J and Whelan, B (1997), *Clean & Competitive: Motivating Environmental Performance in Industry*, Earthscan, London.

Schaltegger, S & Burritt, R (2000), *Contemporary Environmental Accounting: Issues, Concepts and Practice,* Greenleaf Publishing, Sheffield, UK.

United Nations Statistical Division (1993), *Handbook on Integrated Environmental and Economic Accounting, Studies in methods,* Series F, No. 61, United Nations, New York.

World Business Council for Sustainable Development (WBCSD), (1997), *Environmental Performance and Shareholder Value*, Geneva.

Appendices

Appendices

Appendix 1 – Disentangling the definitions

Sustainability and sustainable development

Sustainability

Sustainability may best be defined as the 'capacity for continuance into the long-term future'. Anything that can go on being done on an indefinite basis is sustainable. Anything that cannot go on being done indefinitely is unsustainable. In that respect, sustainability is the end goal, or desired destination, for the human species as much as for any other species.

Sustainable development

By contrast, sustainable development is the process by which we move towards sustainability. There have been many attempts to define sustainable development, the most widely used of which is the definition that first appeared in the Brundtland Report back in 1987: 'Development that meets the needs of the present without compromising the ability of future generations to meet their own needs.' But the limitations of this definition are becoming more and more obvious. It fails to convey the idea that there are biophysical limits within which society must operate, if the ecological capital on which we depend is not to be eroded – limits that the environmental accounting methodology described in this guide attempt to apply to individual organisations. Forum for the Future uses the following alternative: 'Sustainable development is a dynamic process which enables all people to realise their potential and to improve their quality of life in ways which simultaneously protect and enhance the Earth's life support systems.'

This definition affirms sustainable development as a dynamic process and emphasises the importance of social justice and equity in that it is for all people. It also makes it clear that achieving sustainable development is not simply about manipulating the environment, while people pursue their business as usual. It is a social and economic project as much as an environmental project, and one with the very positive objective of optimising human well-being.

Appendix 2 – The Forum's Five Capitals Model

As explained in Appendix 1, sustainability may best be defined as the capacity for continuance into the long-term future. Anything that can go on being done on an indefinite basis is sustainable. Anything that cannot go on being done indefinitely is unsustainable.

In terms of the human species, we are first and foremost dependent on sustaining those biophysical systems which allow life on earth to continue. Beyond that perhaps the most helpful way of understanding sustainability is in terms of the economic concepts of capital and income. Sustainability depends upon maintaining, and where possible, increasing the stocks of the five capital assets described below, so that we succeed in living off the income without depleting the capital.

Natural capital (also referred to as environmental or ecological capital) is any stock or flow of energy and matter that yields valuable goods and services. It falls into several categories:

- resources, some of which are renewable (timber, grain, fish and water), whilst others are not (fossil fuels);
- sinks which absorb, neutralise or recycle wastes; and
- processes, such as climate regulation.

Natural capital is the basis not only of production but of life itself.

Human capital consists of health, knowledge, skills and motivation, all of which are required for productive work. Enhancing human capital (for instance, through investment in education and training) is central to a flourishing economy. Poverty is both morally indefensible and socially inefficient in that it prevents millions of people from fulfilling their potential and becoming engaged in the creation of wealth.

Social capital is the value added to any activity or economic process by human relationships and co-operation. Social capital takes the form of structures or institutions that enable individuals to maintain and develop their human capital in partnership with others and includes families, communities, businesses, trade unions, schools, and voluntary organisations.

Manufactured capital comprises material goods – tools, machines, buildings, and other forms of infrastructure – that contribute to the production process, but do not become embodied in its output.

Financial capital plays an important role in our economy, by reflecting the productive power of the other types of capital and enabling them to be owned and traded. However, unlike the other types, it has no intrinsic value; whether in shares, bonds or banknotes, its value is purely representative of natural, human, social or manufactured capital.

At the heart of the current environmental crisis is the way in which present patterns of consumption and production are unsustainably depleting environmental capital, such that its ability to support the projected levels of the human population in the next century at all (let alone at the standard of living of most people in the affluent industrialised companies) is seriously brought into question. As Paul Hawken and Amory Lovins argue in *Natural Capitalism* (1999):

'What might be called "industrial capitalism" does not fully conform to its own accounting principles. It liquidates its capital and calls it income. It neglects to assign any value to the largest stocks of capital it employs, the natural resources and living systems, as well as the social and cultural systems that are the basis of human capital.'

Forum for the Future advocates a model of sustainable capitalism, based around maintaining and, where possible, increasing our stocks of these different capital assets, so that we succeed in living off the income without depleting the capital. They are the capital stocks from which we have to derive all our goods and services, and produce improvements in human welfare and quality of life. If consumption is at the expense of investment, then such consumption is not sustainable and will inevitably be reduced in the future.

However, it is worth bearing in mind that all such categorisations are more than a little arbitrary. In reality, there are only two sources of wealth in the world today: the wealth that flows from our use of the earth's resources and ecosystems, all powered by incoming solar radiation (our natural capital); and the wealth that flows from the use of our hands, brains and spirits (our human capital). All else – money, machines, institutions, etc. – is a derivative of these two primary sources of wealth.

Appendix 3: Data Entry (Green) Sheets

Environmentally-related data required to produce corporate environmental external cost accounts

Please note these sheets also capture environmentally-related financial data that may already be captured (but perhaps lost) within the company's financial accounting system/the nominal ledger.

Table 1: Direct energy use

Type of energy	kWh *or other units please specify*	Total financial cost	General ledger account number	Cost per kWh/litre, etc.
Gas/natural gas				
Electricity:				
From renewable sources				
• (please specify type)*				
Non-renewable/fossil				
fuel sources				
CHP – please provide details				
Fuel oil/gas oil/diesel				
Propane				
Other (please specify)				

Notes
- Please specify data sources and also details of any assumptions made or estimated figures disclosed.
- Total financial cost should be the total energy/utility bill, i.e. including all standing charges and rentals.
- Electricity obtained under a green tariff/guaranteed renewable source should be disclosed separately in the above table, if known, please detail source of renewable energy, e.g. wind, landfill gas, biomass, etc.

Potential sources of information:
- Utility bills, supplier bills, etc.

Table 2: Company cars

Fuel type	No. of vehicles	Total kms	Total fuel consumption (litres)	Total fuel cost (please specify currency)	General ledger account number	Average fuel efficiency (kms/litres)
Petrol						
Diesel						
Low sulphur/ city diesel						
Other (please specify)						
Totals						

Notes
- Please specify data sources and also details of any assumptions made or estimated figures disclosed in the above table.
- Please provide as much details as possible – ideally a listing of all cars detailing the registration, vehicle type, driver (not necessary), kms, fuel used and total fuel cost.
- Other fuel types could include electric vehicles (EVs) or liquid petroleum gas (LPG) or compressed natural gas (CNG).

Potential sources of information:
- Fuel cards, leasing company records, etc.

Table 2A: Distribution fleet

Fuel type	No. of vehicles	Total kms	Total fuel consumption *(litres)*	Total fuel cost *(please specify currency)*	General ledger account number	Average fuel efficiency *(kms/litres)*
Petrol						
Diesel						
Low sulphur/ city diesel						
Other (please specify)						
Totals						

Notes

Please state number of vehicles by class of vehicle by type, i.e. artic, rigid truck, panel van and so on. Please also state mileage per year per vehicle and what EU class it is – Euro I, Euro II, Euro III.

Table 3: Air travel (summary table)

Total kms flown	Total cost of air travel	General ledger account number
Totals		

Notes

Total company air miles need to be determined for the year/accounting period under review. This data should be available directly from your travel agent/s. Ideally they should be able to provide a detailed list of destinations flown to, number of times that destination was flown to and the total mileage flown, i.e. destinations times number of occasions that route was flown. This data will be needed every year so ideally you should ask your travel agent to begin to collate it routinely. If this is not possible this year please provide what you can, e.g. number of short haul and number of long haul flights, total cost of air travel, etc.

Sources of data:
- Travel agents records.
- Travel agents invoices.

If you have/can get hold of the detail, please complete, in addition to the above table, the table below – you will need to complete most of this to fill in Table 3.

Table 4: Air travel (detail)

Destination – departure and arrival points	Flight cost (total per journey)	Total mileage/kms (please specify miles/kms)	General ledger account number
E.g. London Heathrow to Brussels, Cape Town or wherever			
Totals (where applicable)			

Other transport-related information needs: third party distributions

For completeness and to get a 'true and fair' view of a company's total transport-related impact it is necessary to estimate total road miles incurred by third party carriers. One possible way of doing this would be to go back to the relevant carriers and see if they can provide the total mileage covered by their fleet over the relevant period and an approximation for the proportion of that mileage attributable to your company.

It will also be necessary to find out the fuel type, make and model, and age of a typical third party vehicle or types of vehicles. Emissions can then be estimated on the basis of standard emission coefficients for each class. For example, Euro I panel derived van, Euro II artics, and so on.

Table 5: Personnel commuting travel

Mode of transport	Number of people	Average return journey/ daily commute kms	Average return journey/ Average return journey travel time (hours)	Average weekly distance (kms)	Average annual distance (kms) (47/48 week year)
Car					
Motorbike					
Bus					
Bicycle					
Walk					
Other					
Totals					

This data needs to be collected to get a more accurate and complete estimate of a company's environmental/ecological footprint. Given the fact that a full survey may not be feasible/practical, data may have to be estimated based on an appropriate and representative sample.

Notes

- Account needs to be made of people car sharing, i.e. to avoid double counting.
- Provision also needs to be made for people who travel to work by more than one mode of transport, e.g. drive to local station and then walk/get a bus for the final stage of their journey.
- Account also needs to be taken for part-time workers.

Table 6: Waste and waste management

Type of waste	Qty generated per year (tonnes)	Qty recycled per year (tonnes)	Qty sent to landfill per year (tonnes)	Qty incinerated per year (tonnes)	Sales revenue generated	General ledger account number	Estimated costs of disposal	General ledger account number
Paper								
Cardboard								
Plastic								
Aluminium								
Other materials – please specify								
Totals (where applicable)								

Please quantify/estimate the total quantities of waste being generated annually and provide a rough estimate of the breakdown of this waste – paper/card/plastic/aluminium, etc. Please also note any sales of waste for recycling or quantities of waste by category collected/given away for recycling.

Table 7: Drinking process water

Source of water	Quantity of water used (cubic metres)	Cost per cubic metre	General ledger account number
Mains supply			
Borehole			
Other			
Totals			

Table 8: Waste water

Quantity of waste water discharged to sewer/ water course	Cost per cubic metre of waste water	Total disposal costs	General ledger account number
Totals			

Appendix 4: Pro-forma expense form

Name _A. Smith_ **Period Claimed For:** **From** _6 May 2002_ **To** _23 June 2002_

Date incurred	Brief description of expenditure	Rcpt Y/N*	Program code	Cost code	Analysis code	Recharge-able? Y/N	Names of those travelling	Est. distance (miles)	Cost
								Travel expenses†	
	Travel								
6 May	Rail travel – London to Cheltenham return	Y	SO1	6201			A Smith	240	80.50
8 May	Tube travel – Old Street to London Bridge	Y	S12	6202			A Smith	3	2
	Rail – London to Gatwick	Y	S12	6201			A Smith	30	14.40
	Flight – London – Rome	Y	S12	6203			A Smith	600	240.85
	Bus – Rome A'port to City Centre	N	S12	6206			A Smith	12	2.50
9 May	Taxi – hotel to meetings	Y	S12	6204			A Smith	7	10.00
14 May	Car hire – London – Church Farm, Norfolk	Y	S12	6220			A Smith & F Evans	300	30.00
14 May	Petrol	Y	S12	6210					50.00
	Other expenditure								
May 8/9	Hotel	Y	S12	6230					100.00
May 8/9	Subsistence	Y	S12	6240					38.00
								Total	568.25

Claimant   Date

Budget holder   Date

For Accounts use

Cheque No/
BPS ref. No./
Petty Cash Folio No./

Index

Index

Environmental Cost Accounting: an Introduction and Practical Guide

First published in 2002 by:

The Chartered Institute of Management Accountants

26 Chapter Street

London

SW1P 4NP

ISBN 1 85971 537 0

Printed in Great Britain

The publishers of this book consider that it is a worthwhile contribution to discussion, without neces-sarily sharing the views expressed, which are those of the author.

No responsibility for loss occasioned to any person acting or refraining from action as a result of any material in this publication can be accepted by the authors or publishers.